DEALING WITH AGGRESSION AND VIOLENCE IN YOUR WORKPLACE

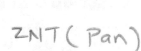

Other titles in the Successful LIS Professional series

THE SUCCESSFUL **LIS** PROFESSIONAL

SERIES EDITOR
Sheila Pantry

DEALING WITH AGGRESSION AND VIOLENCE IN YOUR WORKPLACE

Sheila Pantry, OBE

LIBRARY ASSOCIATION PUBLISHING
LONDON

© Sheila Pantry 1996

Published by
Library Association Publishing
7 Ridgmount Street
London WC1E 7AE

First published 1996

British Library Cataloguing in Publication Data
A catalogue record for this book is available from the British Library

ISBN 1-85604-180-8

Typeset in 11/14 pt Aldine 721 by Library Association Publishing.
Printed and made in Great Britain by Biddles Ltd, Guildford, Surrey.

Contents

Series Editor's preface

With rapid technological advances and new freedoms, the workplace presents a dynamic and challenging environment. It is just these advances, however, that necessitate a workforce relying on its versatility and adaptability knowing that life-long full-time jobs are a thing of the past. Work is being contracted out, de-structured organizations are emerging and different skills and approaches are required from 'brain-workers' who must solve new and changing problems. All workers must become self-motivated, multi-skilled and constantly learning. Demonstrating the international economic importance of professional development, the European Commission has officially voiced its commitment to a European community committed to lifelong learning.

For the information professional, the key to success in this potentially de-stabilizing context is to develop the new skills the workplace demands. Above all, the LIS professional must actively prioritize a commitment to continuous professional development. The information industry is growing fast and the LIS profession is experiencing very rapid change. This series has been designed to help you manage change by prioritizing the growth of your own portfolio of professional skills. By reading these books you will have begun the process of seeing yourself as your own best resource and begun the rewarding challenge of staying ahead of the game.

The series is a very practical one, focusing on specific topics relevant to all types of library and information service. Recognizing that your time is precious, these books have been written so that they may be easily read and digested. They include instantly applicable ideas and techniques which you can put to the test in your own workplace, helping you to succeed in your job.

The authors have been selected because of their practical experience and enthusiasm for their chosen topic and we hope you will benefit from their advice and guidance. The points for reflection, checklists and summaries are designed to provide stepping stones for you to assess your understanding of the topic as you read.

As an information professional who is extremely keen on professional development at any age I recommend this series to you. I am positive you will benefit from your investment!

Sheila Pantry

Acknowledgements

I appreciate the help given to me while compiling this book – the staff of Library Association Publishing, Victim Support, our wonderful police force and various colleagues including Richard Proctor of the University of Sheffield, Department of Information Studies and George Evers of the Netherlands Institute for the Working Environment NIA.

In particular, I thank my husband for reading the script and listening to my ideas during the writing and to Katherine Chambers who word-processed the script, I hope that all her future workplaces will be safe and healthy!

Glossary

Acronyms and abbreviations used in the text

CISDOC	International Labour Office Health and Safety Centre's database
EC	European Commission
EU	European Union
HASAWA	The Health and Safety at Work etc. Act 1974
HSC	Health and Safety Commission
HSE	Health and Safety Executive
HSELINE	Health and Safety Executive Information Services database
ILO	International Labour Office (in Geneva)
MHSW	The Management of Health and Safety Regulations 1992
NIOSH	National Institute of Occupational Safety and Health (in USA)
NIOSHTIC	National Institute of Occupational Safety and Health databases
OSH	Occupational Safety and Health
RIDDOR	Reporting of Injuries, Diseases and Dangerous Occurrences Regulations 1995

Introduction

Many people who work in information centres and libraries suffer, often in silence, from aggression, bullying, harassment and violence.

This book is written from the viewpoint of health and safety at work practice. Although people's views on standards of acceptable behaviour are likely to differ, it is vital that consensus is reached in each workplace. It makes it much easier for you and your colleagues to act if you have a clear idea of what should and should not be tolerated.

The first chapter includes a collection of incidents which have happened to colleagues in various information centres and libraries here in the United Kingdom. The stories do not make happy reading, but are put there to alert you to the fact that you could have been such a victim. Chapter 2 explains to you the current concerns, why information centres and libraries are targets; the various definitions of aggression, from bullying – verbal and nonverbal – through to physical violence. Chapter 3 asks if you are at risk and will give you enough information to decide, if you do have problems, how to get your management to take action.

In Chapter 4 you are introduced to risk assessment which is the key to procuring a healthy and safe working environment. It tells you what your management's legal responsibilities are and introduces you to the steps which should be taken to assess the risks. Once the overall picture has been gained on whether or not a problem exists, you must ensure that your management accepts that there is a problem.

Chapter 5 – 'Taking action', shows you how to investigate, which preventative measures should be taken, and the reporting procedures and checks which should be in place to ensure that all is working well! Chapter 6 looks at the training – the 'what, where and how' – and offers guidance as to what is available for you. Examples of training videos and films which may help you are cited in Appendix E. Finally Chapter 7 explains to you what support should be available to you if unfortunately you are involved in an incident. I have included a short glossary at the beginning to help you with some of the terminology and acronyms used.

The appendices to the book include a bibliography to enable you to read more widely on the subject; a list of legislation which applies to workplaces; details of various databases, both online and in CD-ROM format, which provide even more bibliographic citations and also full text of some of the legislation and guidance quoted. The last two appendices give you contacts for help and an example of an anti-harassment policy.

I hope this book and the other publications and training opportunities listed in it will help you to work in an environment which is healthy and safe.

Chapter 1
Aggressive and violent incidents in information centres and libraries

In this chapter you will:

➤ learn about the current concerns on aggression and violence
➤ find examples of incidents of aggression and violence which have occurred in information centres and libraries
➤ learn how aggression and violence have affected people like you working in information centres and libraries.

Introduction

It is a daunting thought that during the course of your work today you may experience some form of aggression or bullying or may even suffer a violent incident.

The current concern in the media – in newspapers and magazines, on the TV and radio – shows that in recent years there has been a significant increase in the amount of vandalism, aggressive behaviour and bullying everywhere, including information centres and libraries. What is even more worrying is the growth in the number of abusive or violent attacks on members of information and library staff, and the way in which such behaviour affects other information centre and library users.

While it is not the role of staff or employers to solve the underlying problems of violence in our society, it is clear that there is a lot individuals and organizations can do to reduce the risk of violence. Judging by the evidence which has accumulated, many library authorities and organizations are already regarding the matter seriously and devising their own preventative measures. Advice, guidance and various procedures which can be adapted to local situations where a problem exists, or is thought to exist, can be found in this book and in other publications listed in the bibliography in Appendix A. They should also sound a cautionary note to those who do not have an acknowledged problem. This book is aimed at individual staff members in all types of information centres and libraries, but managers, trade unionists, health and safety supervisors, chief officers, elected members and owners should all benefit from reading it.

Most people believe that an accident or incident will not happen to them, but the following incidents have really happened to colleagues in the profession here in the United Kingdom (UK). They do not make pleasant reading, but I feel you should be aware of them. If, after reading this book you believe that you are not properly trained then you should make sure that you go on a training course so you are prepared should any acts of aggression, violence or harassment happen to you.

These incidents may also be used as a focal point for the setting up of staff discussion groups to raise awareness and perhaps find out if there are any problems in your particular information centre or library. Some of these incidents do not offer solutions, some tell of the consequences and others of actions taken.

Incident 1

Five minutes before the library was due to close, a library assistant in a suburban branch library was approached by a man wishing to renew two books.

One of the books was two days overdue and was also required by another reader. The library assistant politely informed the man that the book could not be renewed.

The man tried to reason with the assistant, arguing that if he had kept the book another three days he could have finished it and the fine would have been the same. He asked for the book back, saying he no longer wished to return it.

The assistant said that he could not agree to his retaining the book. The book had been discharged and he would have to reserve it. The man exploded with anger and verbally abused the assistant. He demanded the book back, and when she refused, he came behind the counter and knocked the assistant back from the counter with his arm. He took the book and left the library. Unfortunately no further action was taken, but the assistant was very upset and nervous for some time afterwards.

Incident 2

A young female assistant in an inner-city library was approached by two teenage youths. Grinning and nudging one another, they asked her if she could show them some books with pictures of people having sex.

The assistant told them there were no books like that in the library. The youths persisted, asking her to find them some novels with sex scenes in them. The assistant refused.

The youths became increasingly boisterous, picking up scissors and pencils from the counter, and throwing them to each other.

The assistant told them to leave the library. They abused her verbally, and as they left, one of them picked up a pair of scissors and lunged at the assistant, cutting her hand.

This incident, the worst of many instances of threatening behaviour, led to the temporary evening closure of the library. The closure was made permanent three months later.

Incident 3

A small suburban public library had been having trouble with teenage rowdyism for some months. The police were often called, but the culprits had always left by the time they arrived.

One evening, the librarian's patience broke. The library was empty, except for the troublemakers. As soon as she had called the police she left the library and locked the doors behind her, to make sure they would be there when the police came.

As soon as the youths realized what she had done, they began trying to break out of the library attacking the thick glass door with chairs. When this failed, they rampaged through the library, causing considerable damage. They eventually broke out of the library staff exit, and left shouting threats at the librarian. Again no action was taken.

Incident 4

An inner-city library was regularly used in the evening by a gang of a dozen or more youths to meet their girlfriends, and in winter, to keep warm.

In order to avoid a major confrontation the group was tolerated. Only when they grew particularly rowdy, throwing books around the library, were they asked to leave. This they usually did, although the assistants had to put up with much verbal abuse from one individual, known as Jake, who often refused to go until he knew the police had been called.

One evening after the gang had been particularly disruptive the police were called from the library office and when they arrived, the gang was severely reprimanded and dispersed.

Half an hour later Jake returned and shouted to the assistants that he would get even with them for calling the police.

The following evening, he returned to the library and produced a sawn-off shotgun from under his coat. He terrorized the staff for several minutes, threatening to shoot them, until he eventually left of his own accord.

After the incident a meeting of community leaders took place. Jake was caught and temporarily taken into care. He was found to be seriously disturbed, probably schizophrenic. After some months he was released back into the community.

Soon afterwards the library installed a security lock, operated from the counter. The library is now kept locked in the evenings. Tables have been removed and chairs reduced to the minimum to make the library less attractive for 'social' activities.

Incident 5

A female reference library assistant was working on the counter one winter's evening. During the evening she noticed a scruffy-looking man in his thirties sitting at a desk not far from the counter. He had a newspaper in front of him, but whenever she looked his way, he seemed to be watching her. Over a period of about two hours, whenever she looked at him, his eyes were on her.

When the library closed at 8pm, the man left. Uneasy about the unwanted attention she had been getting, the assistant asked a colleague to accompany her to the bus station. The route passed through a dark, vandalized subway.

The same evening the following week, the assistant was again on duty. She was relieved to find that the man was not in the library.

On her way to the bus station, alone this time, the assistant realized she was being followed. When she quickened her pace, her follower did the same. No physical attack took place, but the assistant was badly shaken, and asked to be relieved of evening duties for a period.

The police were informed but the man was not seen again.

Incident 6

A small suburban library became a second home for a number of unemployed young men, who gathered there after the local pub shut at lunchtime. They were tolerated as long as they did not disturb other users. Occasionally, it was clear they had had too much to drink, and when they became excessively noisy they were asked to leave.

On one occasion an assistant observed one man mimicking the rolling walk of a library user with a severe weight problem.

At an appropriate moment, the assistant approached him and asked him to leave. She told him that his behaviour was unacceptable.

He didn't object, and made his way to the door, accompanied by his friends. On his way past the counter he paused for a moment in front of the assistant and spat over the front of her dress.

The man was reported to the police, who said that they were unable to take action unless the assistant was prepared to press charges. This she was not prepared to do.

The following day, the man apologized to the assistant for his behaviour. He had had, he said, too much to drink.

Incident 7

A member of the public asked for help – he wanted to talk to a religious minister. The library staff member located names and addresses, made some telephone calls on behalf of the customer, who suddenly started to become abusive and aggressive and threw coins at the staff member who tried to calm the situation. On this occasion the customer did calm down.

On a second occasion the same customer again became abusive verbally and then physically tried to hit the staff member. A senior staff member appeared on the scene and after quietening the customer down asked him to leave the premises. The staff member involved in the incident had to be sent home from duty. The next day the staff discussed the problem and eventually panic buttons were given to the staff.

Incident 8

A staff member in a large town's central library was attacked by a man in the entrance who had set off the security system. The man was arrested, tried by jury and found guilty. A three-month prison sentence was given, but two months of this were suspended. Because of the length of time the man was held in custody, he actually only spent about two weeks in prison – but he did go to prison.

Incident 9

A security man of a large central public library was assaulted by a member of the public (a well-known down and out) who was trying to enter the library, despite already being banned from the library because of his aggressive manner towards both the staff and other members of the public. He had been a nuisance for many years and indeed still is! The security man received cuts and bruises to his mouth and lost some teeth in the fracas. The man causing the disturbance was arrested, released on bail after being assessed by social workers and deemed not a threat to the public, although an injunction was imposed – banning him from coming within a hundred yards of the library while the matter was dealt with.

The security man did pursue compensation through the Criminal Injuries Compensation Board and it was awarded.

Another incident involving the same man took place less than two years later when he threatened a staff member at the entrance with a cricket bat. The police were called, but were unable to act as the man had disappeared by the time they arrived.

Points to reflect on . . .

➤ Would you have known what to do in these incidents?
➤ Have similar incidents occurred in your information centre or library?
➤ If so, did you report them to your management?

Chapter 2
What is work-related aggression and violence?

In this chapter you will find information on:

➤ why information centres and libraries are targets
➤ definitions and causes of aggression from bullying – verbal and non-verbal – to physical violence
➤ which pieces of legislation can be used to seek improvements in information centres and libraries.

Why information centres and libraries?

Information centres and libraries tend to be places which are easily accessible, warm, informal and welcoming. The Library Association in its pamphlet on *Violence in libraries: preventing aggressive and unacceptable behaviour in libraries*, June 1987, states:

> The success of the service very often depends on these attributes – but this same openness can mean that staff are vulnerable in the face of anti-social behaviour. It is important not to lose sight of the positive aspects of library and information services when considering the subject of violence, but nevertheless forward planning and good management practices can avoid or alleviate situations where staff find themselves in danger, or afraid or unable to cope.

Work-related aggression and violence is an increasing problem for many people and many different work groups. Perception of what is, and what is not, an act of violence depends on many factors, including the relative vulnerability of the people involved.

Employers need to be able to show evidence that they are taking steps to look after their employees – Section 2 of the Health and Safety at Work etc. Act 1974 gives employers a duty of care to their staff and the public, and the Management of Health and Safety at Work Regulations 1992 require employers to undertake risk assessment which includes risk of violence. The revised Reporting of Injuries, Diseases and Dangerous Occurrences Regulations (RIDDOR) 1995 specifically requires the reporting of workplace violence.

Aggression and violence at work is not a unique problem to the UK: a survey of the major occupational health and safety databases – **HSE-LINE** from the United Kingdom Health and Safety Executive Information Services, **CISDOC** from the International Labour Office Health and Safety Centre, and **NIOSHTIC** from the United States National Institution of Occupational Safety and Health – reveals a growing concern over workplace violence around the world. In particular the literature shows that authorities and organizations in Australia, Canada, Ireland, New Zealand, The Netherlands, South Africa, Sweden, and the USA have already recognized the problems and are taking action.

So what is work-related aggression and violence?

At a recent European Commission Expert meeting on work-related violence the following definition of violent incidents was offered:

> incidents where persons are abused, threatened or assaulted in circumstances relating to their work, involving an implicit or explicit challenge to their safety, well-being or health

The UK Health and Safety Executive, the Government Agency responsible for securing health and safety at work, similarly defines violence to staff at work as:

> any incident in which an employee is abused, threatened or assaulted by a member of the public in circumstances arising out of the course of his/her employment. (Health and Safety Executive, 1988)

There is now a specific requirement to report workplace violence in the newly revised RIDDOR (see above for details) which states it to be 'an act of non-consensual physical violence done to a person at work'. You

9

should also be aware that aggression and violence can be between employees and also between employee and managers.

The Library Association states in the pamphlet cited above that 'the term "violence in libraries" can be seen as shorthand for describing all sorts of anti-social behaviour, ranging from spitting, damaging furniture or playing radios, to theft, verbal abuse and physical attack'.

The Swedish National Board of Occupational Safety and Health defines the problem as 'recurrent reprehensible or distinctly negative actions which are directed against individual employees in an offensive manner and can result in those employees being placed outside the workplace community'. (Sweden National Board of Occupational Safety and Health, ordinance on victimization at work, AFS, 1993:7)

MSF, the UK union for skilled and professional people defines bullying as 'persistent, offensive, abusive, intimidating, malicious or insulting behaviour, abuse of power or unfair penal sanctions, which makes the recipient feel upset, threatened, humiliated or vulnerable, which undermines their self-confidence and which may cause them to suffer stress' (MSF, 1995).

These definitions may not quite fit your workplace. If not, it may be useful to talk over and agree an alternative with your employer and other colleagues.

Types of aggression and violence in the workplace

These can take the following forms:

➤ verbal abuse or a threatening attitude from a customer, colleague or manager;
➤ threat of assault, particularly with a weapon;
➤ actual assault which can result in physical injury or sexual assault.

The ways in which aggression manifests itself can be illustrated as follows:

➤ using terror tactics, open aggression, threats, shouting abuse and obscenities, sexual or ethnic harassment;
➤ constant humiliation, ridicule or belittling efforts, often in front of others;

➤ interpersonal conflicts between staff or between managers/supervisors and staff;
➤ excessive supervision, monitoring everything that is done;
➤ being excessively critical about minor things;
➤ withholding information so that a person cannot do a job effectively;
➤ removing areas of responsibility from a person or constantly overruling a person's authority;
➤ constant blocking of reasonable requests for leave, training or a person's promotion;
➤ customers making unreasonable requests and then creating a scene in front of work colleagues and other customers;
➤ intruders or customers creating a disturbance in the library or information centre.

What causes aggression and violence?

There are many reasons why aggression of any kind occurs in libraries or information centres. Easy access, long opening hours and friendly, helpful staff all contribute to making libraries and information centres seem welcoming and attractive places to visit. But this in itself can mean that staff are vulnerable, as acts of aggression and violence or generally anti-social behaviour can erupt without warning in today's violent society. Increased pressures on the workforce to improve productivity, delayering of staff and financial cutbacks resulting in reduced staff numbers can all contribute to the increase in aggression among both staff and customers. The following also cause problems:

➤ antagonistic behaviour by customers who oppose any authoritative regime, e.g. restrictions on the number of books which can be borrowed at any one time; imposing a fine for late return of the books; calling closing time when the customer wants to stay longer;
➤ lack of respect for others and their points of view;
➤ excessive or inflexible workloads and demands on people;
➤ targets not clearly defined or impossible deadlines;
➤ poor working relationships and conflict between individuals including possibly sexual or racial harassment;

11

➤ no clear code of policy or conduct;

➤ organizational change and uncertainty;

➤ styles of management and supervision which may encourage aggressive behaviour in the mistaken belief that it is 'strong' management;

➤ one section trying to get work from another section in order to survive.

It is also possible that aggressive behaviour between individuals and groups can be caused by the physical conditions of the working environment, such as excessive noise and vibration, heat, humidity or other obvious workplace hazards which might not be adequately controlled.

Whose concern is it?

Both employer and employees have an interest in reducing violence at work. For employers, violence can lead to low morale and a poor image for the organization, making it difficult to recruit staff (see also Chapter 3, p. 17). It can also mean extra costs, with absenteeism, higher insurance premiums and compensation payments. For you as an employee, violence can cause pain, suffering and even disability or death. Physical attacks are obviously dangerous but serious or persistent verbal abuse or threats can also damage employees' health through anxiety or stress.

There are some pieces of legislation which can be used to seek improvements in the workplace, which are described below. *You should note that in the legislation quoted, where the term 'He or him' is used, in legal terminology the law applies to both the male and female genders.*

All employers have a legal duty under section 2(1) of the Health and Safety at Work etc Act 1974 to ensure, 'so far as is reasonably practicable, the health, safety and welfare at work of their employees'. This duty can extend to protecting employees from assaults, aggression, bullying and other stressful situations. Every employer also has a legal duty to make a sufficient and suitable assessment of the risks to health and safety of their employees to which they are exposed while at work, so that appropriate preventative and protective measures can be introduced.

You should also be aware that under section S2(6) of the UK Health and Safety at Work etc. Act 1974 and under Regulation 4A of the Safety Representatives and Safety Committees Regulations 1977 employers have a duty to consult trade union Safety Representatives about health and safety matters. (For readers in other countries find out what your health and safety legislation prescribes.) See Chapter 4 for more details on management responsibilities.

From reports and articles in the press and literature it can be seen that there are many causes and effects of violent behaviour – some may be easy to identify, such as frustration, anger, misunderstanding, stress, communication problems, conflict with authority and theft or robbery. Other manifestations such as workplace aggression and bullying or racial and sexual discrimation may be harder to identify, prove and bring to the notice of managers, because these types of incident usually occur on a one-to-one basis. Providing evidence that such incidents have occurred can cause anguish for the person on the receiving end of them, because often a more senior member of staff may be responsible for the acts of aggression, bullying or discrimination.

Guidance and advice is abundant, and employers, in collaboration with the employees, will need to carry out a risk assessment and develop, within the information centre or library safety policy, proposed actions to tackle aggression and violence at work. Such a policy and the means to carry it out will need the support and cooperation of all staff, so consultation with management, supervisors, security, personnel, the safety officer, staff and union safety representatives is essential. Therefore, employers must heed the requirements of the legislation and secure a safe working environment for all those working in information centres and libraries. And employees must cooperate.

Being constantly alert

You need to be aware at all times that people you meet on a daily basis in your library or information centre can become excited and reveal tensions and inhibitions hitherto unrevealed. This may have repercussions and the chances of verbal and perhaps physical abuse may increase.

An outburst may or may not be the direct result of interaction with yourself but perhaps stems from a request being made which cannot be immediately fulfilled. This may add to some in-built frustration already being experienced by the individual making the request and as a result you may experience a violent or abusive situation (e.g. Chapter 1, Incident 1).

So it is necessary to learn how to react and you should be aware that perhaps a downright unsympathetic attitude may result in increased frustration and anger which could degenerate into a violent situation.

You should also be aware that there may be incidents where a person's behaviour may be impossible to analyse, but you do need to be trained in how to alleviate such situations or indeed prevent them from getting worse.

Training is essential because it will help you to identify the possible causes, and provide you with information and skills on how to avoid such situations. If they do occur you will be better equipped to deal with potentially violent situations. There is more information on training in Chapter 6.

Points to reflect on . . .

➤ **Do you understand the various forms of aggression and violence which can occur in information centres and libraries?**
➤ **Does your employer have a health and safety policy?**
➤ **Are you now aware of the legislation which exists to protect you at work?**

Chapter 3
Are you at risk?

In this chapter you will find information to help you:

➤ understand how aggression and violence can affect you physically and mentally
➤ decide if there is a problem
➤ encourage your management to take action.

Making sure you are safe

Considering risks should be part of your everyday thinking and you should appreciate that risks at work do not exist just at your desk, counter, or in your library or information centre. There may be risks in travelling to and from work or in connection with your work; in work that you might do on someone else's premises; or in car parks, lifts, corridors, etc. You should be aware that work-related risks may occur in time spent away from home or when travelling abroad.

The legislation requires employers to secure the personal safety of their employees, but you should remember that personal safety is a shared responsibility between employer and employee, so you also have a responsibility to help yourself be safer.

You should also think about the personal safety of others: family, colleagues, work contacts and friends. Acquiring skills and strategies should become almost instinctive, so that if a difficult – and potentially violent – situation arises, you have the confidence to know what to do. (See Chapter 6 on training.)

How aggression and violence can affect you

Both immediate and long-term effects may result from aggression, bullying and violence. You should be aware of the following repercussions.

Psychological effects

Victims of violent behaviour lose 'self-confidence' and their self-esteem, and risk suffering stress. This, if not adequately treated, may further develop into behavioural problems of anxiety or depression.

Physical effects

An injury may need treatment including surgery. Serious injuries have led to long-term disability, and the possibility of not being able to carry on with a career.

Stress and its effects

Continuous pressures or other types of excessive demands place a great deal of stress on individuals. Stress is associated with a wide range of ill-health and can affect you in a number of ways.

Stress-related physical effects

Headaches/migraine, dizziness, raised heart beat, sweating, blurred vision, loss of appetite, inability to sleep, skin diseases, sickness, irritable bowels, aching neck and shoulders, lowering of resistance to infection.

Stress-related psychological and behavioural effects

Anxiety and irritability, depression, poor concentration, tendency to consume more alcohol and tobacco, tearfulness, inability to deal with everyday tasks and situations in a calm/controlled manner.

You should be aware that the effects of stress are usually short-lived and cause no lasting harm if the pressures are short-lived. However, you should be warned that where pressures are intense and continuous for some time, the effects of such stress can be far more sustained, leading eventually to longer-term psychological problems and physical ill-health.

The Health and Safety Executive warn that stress is associated with a number of serious ill-health conditions such as high blood pressure, thyroid disorders, ulcers, heart disease, anxiety and depression.

All this can have a secondary effect on the success of the library or information centre's services, can create a bad atmosphere which affects customers and could, if you are in a 'business-oriented service', lead to a loss of business with the attendant loss of sales and profit to consider. If staff loss through resignation is involved, then this in turn could add to staff costs by the need to recruit and retrain valuable staff. The loss of staff in itself can put extra pressure and stress on the staff who remain and could cause some further aggression. Repeated failure to respond to staff complaints could possibly result in a Constructive Dismissal claim, which may result in public exposure through cases being taken to Industrial Tribunals and reported in the media.

You as an employee, should be aware that employers need to be able to show evidence that they are taking steps to look after their staff but first of all it will be necessary to find out if there is a problem.

Is there a problem?

Your employer may think that aggression and violence is not a problem at your workplace or that incidents are rare. However, *you as an employee* may have a different view.

The easiest way to find out is to ask your colleagues. This can be done informally through contact with managers, supervisors, safety representatives or trade union representatives. Alternatively your manager may agree to circulate a questionnaire. The idea is to find out whether you or any colleagues ever feel threatened or under great stress. The results of such a survey should be published so that if there is a problem, everyone will realize that the manager recognizes it, and if there is not, any fears will be allayed.

Even if no problem is found, it is wise to check the position again from time to time, because things can change.

The first steps

The first steps which should be taken in making an assessment of whether aggression and violence exists are:

➤ consult with colleagues;
➤ find out if there is a problem in the workplace;
➤ build up a picture of incidents;
➤ ask management to set up a formal procedure to report any incidents;
➤ classify all incidents;
➤ keep records of incidents where staff are injured as part of your legal duties under Reporting of Injuries, Diseases and Dangerous Occurrences Regulations (RIDDOR);
➤ ensure reports are made;
➤ search for preventative measures;
➤ decide what to do;
➤ put measures into practice.

Record all incidents

It is the duty of your manager to keep a detailed record of all incidents, so a picture can be built up if there is a problem. A simple report form (as suggested by the Health and Safety Executive and the Library Association) can be used to record the details of what happened, where, when and who was involved, and any possible causes (see Chapter 5 for more details and sample forms).

You should be aware that your colleagues may not report incidents for all sorts of reasons. Perhaps they accept aggressive behaviour as part of the job. They may think it will reflect badly on them if they admit it happens.

Sometimes victims of aggression are often unable to recognize the unfair treatment they are receiving. Be aware that some employers are reluctant to admit that any form of aggression is taking place in their organization.

There can be many reasons why incidents are not reported:

➤ where an aggressive management style is in place, staff are afraid to complain in case they are seen to be against management;

➤ some individual incidents may appear trivial, but it is the repetitiveness of these incidents which is important;

➤ men may not want to complain because it may appear unmasculine;

➤ staff are reluctant to complain because there are no witnesses;

➤ victims may feel that any complaint may result in further action by the aggressor;

➤ victims may be afraid to complain because they think management may regard it as being due to their inability to cope.

Therefore, all staff, whatever the level/grade, should be encouraged to report all incidents. Having a report form available will help you and your colleagues to realize that this is what is expected.

Classify all incidents

You, your colleagues and manager will want to know what kinds of incidents are happening. This means classifying them under various headings – place, time, type of incident, who was involved and possible causes.

For example Table 3.1 gives a simple classification to help you decide how serious incidents are.

Table 3.1 Classification of incidents

Type of incident	Result
Involving physical contact	Fatal injury
	Minor injury
	Injury or emotional shock requiring first aid, out-patient treatment, counselling, absence from work (record number of days)
Involving serious or persistent threats of verbal abuse	Emotional shock requiring counselling or absence from work (record number of days)
	Feeling of being at risk or under great stress

It should be easy to classify 'major injuries' but your manager will have to decide how to classify 'serious or persistent verbal abuse' for your organization, so as to cover all incidents that worry staff.

Your manager can use the details on the incident report forms along with the classifications to check for patterns: common causes, work areas, or times of day or night. Remedies can then be targeted where they are needed most. For example, a survey by a trade union after twelve separate shop robberies found that each incident occurred between 5 and 7 o'clock in the evening.

This type of finding may be useful for your management when deciding if security is needed for late night opening of information centres and libraries.

Points to reflect on . . .

➤ Do you think there is a problem of aggression and violence in your workplace?

➤ Do you understand the effects of aggression and violence on the individual?

➤ If, after checking, there is not enough evidence, remember to check again at a later stage

➤ Do you have enough evidence and information to discuss the problem with your management?

➤ You will find more on preventative measures in Chapter 5, pp.28–41.

Chapter 4
The responsibilities of your management

> **In this chapter you will find information on:**
>
> ➤ **the responsibilities of your management**
> ➤ **the concepts of risk assessment**
> ➤ **steps which should be taken in risk assessment.**

You should be aware that it is the duty of every employer under the UK Management of Health and Safety at Work Regulations 1992 to make a suitable and sufficient assessment of:

a)   the risks to the health and safety of his employees to which they are exposed whilst they are at work; and

b)   the risks to health and safety of persons not in his employment arising out of or in connection with the conduct by him of his undertaking, for the purpose of identifying the measures he needs to take to comply with the requirements and prohibitions imposed upon him by or under the relevant statutory provisions.

The Regulations also state:

If you are a self-employed person you will need to make a suitable and sufficient assessment of:

a)   the risks to your own health and safety to which you are exposed whilst you are at a place of work; and

b)   the risks to health and safety of persons not in your employment arising out of or in connection with the conduct by you or your undertaking, for the purpose of identifying the measures you need to take to comply with the requirements and prohibitions imposed upon you by or under the relevant statutory provisions.

Any assessment such as is referred to in the paragraphs above needs to be reviewed, as stated in the same regulations above, by your employer or you as a self-employed person who made the assessment if:

a) there is reason to suspect that it is no longer valid; or

b) there has been a significant change in the matters to which it relates; and where as a result of any such review changes to an assessment are required, the employer or self-employed person concerned shall make them.

Where the employer employs five or more employees, (s)he shall record:

a) the significant findings of the assessment; and

b) any group of his employees identified by it as being especially at risk.

General principles of risk assessment

As stated above, the Management of Health and Safety at Work Regulations require all employers and self-employed persons to make a risk assessment.

Many employers already carry out *de facto* risk assessments on a day-to-day basis during the course of their work; they will note changes in working practice, recognize faults as they develop and take necessary corrective actions. These Regulations, however, require that employers should undertake a systematic general examination of their work activity and that they should record the significant findings of that risk assessment. You should be aware that a risk assessment should usually involve identifying the hazards present in any undertaking (whether arising from work activities or from other factors, e.g. the layout of the library or information centre) and then evaluating the extent of risks involved, taking into account whatever precautions are already being taken. In the UK Health and Safety Executive's Approved Code of the Management of Health and Safety at Work Regulations it states that:

a) a hazard is something with the potential to cause harm (this can include substances or machines, methods of work and other aspects of work organization);

b) risk expresses the likelihood that the harm from a particular hazard is realized;

c) the extent of the risk covers the population which might be affected by a risk, i.e. the number of people who might be affected and the consequences for them.

Risk therefore reflects both the likelihood that harm will occur and its severity.

In some cases, this detailed approach may not be necessary since all the hazards are known and the risks are readily apparent and can therefore be addressed directly.

Purpose of risk assessment

The purpose of the risk assessment is to help the employer or self-employed person to determine what measures should be taken to comply with the employer's or self-employed person's duties under the 'relevant statutory provisions'. This phrase covers the general duties in the Health and Safety at Work etc. Act 1974 (HASAWA) and the more specific duties in the various Acts and Regulations (including these Regulations) associated with the HASAWA.

Regulation 3 of the Management of Health and Safety at Work Regulations does not itself stipulate the measures to be taken as a result of the risk assessment. The measures in each workplace will derive from compliance with other health and safety duties as described above, taking carefully into account the risk assessment. In essence, the risk assessment guides the judgement of the employer or the self-employed person, as to the measures they ought to take to fulfil their statutory obligations.

Steps to risk assessment

Being able to make a judgement about the hazards in your daily life is useful, and the following advice may help when assessing the workplace.

Step 1 – Look for the hazards
If you are doing the assessment yourself, walk around your workplace and look afresh at what could reasonably be expected to cause harm. Ignore the trivial and concentrate only on significant hazards which could result in serious harm or affect several people. Ask your fellow

23

employees or their representatives what they think. They may have noticed things which are not immediately obvious.

Step 2 – Decide who might be harmed, and how
Think about people who may not be in the workplace all the time, e.g. cleaners, visitors, contractors, maintenance personnel, et al. Include members of the public, or people you share your workplace with, if there is a chance they could be hurt by being in or near your activities.

Step 3 – Evaluate the risks arising from the hazards and decide whether existing precautions are adequate or more should be done
Even after all precautions have been taken, some risk usually remains. What you have to decide for *each significant hazard* is whether this remaining risk is high, medium or low. *First*, ask yourself whether your employers have done all the things that the law says they have got to do. For example, there are legal requirements on prevention of access to dangerous parts of machinery. *Then* ask yourself whether generally accepted industry standards are in place. But don't stop there – think for yourself, because the law also says that you must do what is reasonably practicable to keep your workplace safe. Your real aim is to make all risks small by adding to your precautions if necessary. More information about legal requirements and standards can be found in the HSE publications *Management of health and safety at work: approved code of practice* and *Essentials of health and safety*.

If you find that something needs to be done, ask yourself:

(a) Can you and your manager *get rid of the hazard* altogether?
(b) If not, how can you and your manager *control the risks* so that harm is unlikely?

If the work you do tends to vary a lot, or if you or your colleagues move from one site to another, e.g. working in branch libraries or mobile libraries select those hazards which you *can reasonably foresee* and assess the risks from them. After that, if you spot any unusual hazard when you get to a site, get information from others on site, and take what action seems necessary.

If your employer shares a workplace, your employer must tell the other employers and self-employed people there about any risks that the work could cause them, and what precautions are being taken. Also, your manager must think about the risks to you and your colleagues from those who share your workplace.

Step 4 – Record the findings
If your employer has fewer than five employees *s/he does not need to write anything down*, but if there are five or more employees the employer must record the significant findings of the assessment. This means (1) writing down the more significant hazards and (2) recording the most important conclusions. You must also be informed about the findings.

There is no need for your employer to show how s/he did the assessment, provided s/he can show:

➤ that a proper check was made;
➤ *who* might be affected;
➤ that s/he dealt with all the obvious significant hazards, taking into account the *number* of people who could be involved;
➤ that the precautions are reasonable, and the remaining risk is low.

Assessments need to be suitable and sufficient and the following important questions need to be asked:

➤ **Are the precautions reasonable, and**
➤ **Is there something to show that a proper check was made?**

Your employers should keep the written document for future reference or use; it can help if an inspector questions the precautions, or if anyone becomes involved in any action for civil liability. It can also remind you to keep an eye on particular matters. And it helps to show that the employers have done what the law requires. Figure 4.1 shows a sample risk assessment form which you and your employers may find helpful but you may wish to produce your own version tailormade to your specific needs.

Named hazard	What is the risk of injury to employees?	Steps taken (or to take) to avoid injury

Fig. 4.1 *Sample form: Hazard identification and risk assessment – remedial steps*

To make things simpler, you can refer to other documents, such as manuals, the arrangements in the health and safety policy statement, company rules, manufacturers' instructions, and the health and safety procedures. These may already list hazards and precautions. Your employers do not need to repeat all of these in their written documents, and it is up to them whether all the instructions on hazards and precautions are combined altogether in one document, or kept separately.

Step 5 – Review risk assessment from time to time and revise it if necessary
Sooner or later a new layout of the working environment, new equipment, substances and procedures will be introduced which could lead to new problems or hazards. If there is any significant change, these should be added to the assessment to take account of the new problem/ hazard.

In any case it is good practice to review assessments from time to time. Do not amend assessments for trivial change, or still more, for each new job, but if a new job introduces significant new hazards of its own, these need to be considered in their own right and action taken to keep the risks down.

You should also look at Chapters 5 and 6 for details of where improvements in the working environment could be made.

Make sure that your employer plans and organizes work for all employees so as to prevent as reasonably as possible any opportunities for victimization. Also, ensure that there are opportunities to report any emergency unsatisfactory working conditions and steps taken to rectify them.

Your employer will need to implement counter measures without delay if signs of aggression become apparent in any part of the workplace. This should include an investigation of whether the work procedures are the cause.

Most of all, the employer should provide rapid help and support to any victim (see Chapter 7 for further information.)

Points to reflect on . . .

➤ **Do you feel that enough has been done to secure a safe and healthy workplace?**

➤ **Do you understand what a risk assessment is?**

➤ **Has your management done a risk assessment?**

Chapter 5
Taking action

In this chapter you'll find information on:

➤ **what is being done to tackle aggression and violence at work**
➤ **what to do if your manager thinks there is not a problem**
➤ **how to investigate if a problem exists**
➤ **preventative measures**
➤ **reporting procedures**
➤ **checking that procedures work.**

What is being done to combat violence at work?

The European Commission Health and Safety Directorate has instigated some research and its working party will shortly assess the results and make recommendations.

The UK Health and Safety Executive (HSE) has long been concerned and has produced a number of publications which give advice and guidance. A free leaflet *Violence to staff*, IND (G)69 L, gives practical advice to help you find out if there is a problem for staff, and, if it is there, how to tackle it. HSE has also published a priced guidance booklet *Preventing violence to staff* which explains the problem-solving process in more detail and includes case studies that show how it can work in practice. The case studies cover community nursing, pubs, an education authority, a municipal bus company, an ambulance service, London Underground, British Rail, local authority housing and social work departments, but also give scenarios which can offer you guidance and advice on how to tackle the various incidents and problems in any setting.

Recently HSE also published a 38-page booklet *Preventing violence to retail staff*. This booklet gives excellent advice which can be applied to any industry. This guidance booklet will help those developing a company policy and illustrates how to take preventative measures including training of staff. Another very important area is also covered – how to give post-incident support to staff, which should not be seen as a separate issue. Providing support for staff should be part of the overall policy on preventing and controlling violence at work and there is a network of local Victim Support schemes. Victim Support is a national charity providing practical help and information, particularly on the criminal justice system (see page 51).

A search through the occupational health and safety databases such as HSELINE, CISDOC and NIOSHTICS mentioned in Chapter 2 will give a wide range of further guidance and advice which has been produced by organizations worldwide to help combat aggression and violence in the workplace. Have you or your manager *taken all the necessary precautions which will secure a safer working environment for you and other staff*? If not, the following measures suggested by The Library Association in *Violence in libraries* should be considered:

> Different people will have different ideas of what is and is not acceptable behaviour, but consistency in this area is vital. Your management should issue a definition of patterns of unacceptable behaviour, listing these in an easily understood way. It is much easier for you and your colleagues to act if you have a clear idea of what should and should not be tolerated.
>
> If you are working in public libraries, the bye-laws could be used and in schools and colleges the institution's rules could be used as a basis for these definitions. The content and status of the bye-laws and rules should be examined for relevance, currency and legality.
>
> If you work in schools, colleges and universities you should investigate whether or not you are legally protected in the same way as the teaching staff when you are responsible for groups of children/students.
>
> Make sure that the situation over the right to prosecute is clearly understood by all staff, i.e. can an individual decide to prosecute, or can this only be done by senior management or by elected members?
>
> In cases where offenders are under the age for prosecution, the limitations on taking legal actions should be made known to all staff.

If you have a Safety Representative in your library or information service do remember that trade union Safety Representatives have wide-ranging legal rights under the Safety Representatives and Safety Committees Regulations 1977 to investigate potential problems/hazards, inspect workplaces, speak to members in confidence and take up with employers any complaints about health and safety matters. So it is up to you as an individual to share the responsibilities of tackling problems or potential problems of aggression and violence in your workplace.

If your management thinks there is not a problem

Are you sure they understand? Again The Library Association warns:

> There is no point in looking for trouble where it does not exist, but many problems go unreported for a variety of reasons. Some staff accept troublesome behaviour as part of the job, some see it as a personal failure which they do not wish to admit; some have high rates of tolerance. There is also the very real problem of the fear of incidents rather than the active existence of them.

So do not suffer in silence but consider the following action:

Investigate!

The investigation should cover the whole range of aggressive and violent behaviour. You and your colleagues should be consulted to uncover any sort of aggressive or violent incident in which they felt threatened or under stress. It is possible that 'isolated incidents' could prove to be more commonplace than was previously thought. The initial investigations can be carried out by personnel department, occupational health nurses, managers, supervisors, trade union representatives or health and safety supervisors. They can take place as informal interviews or by using questionnaires or forms as suggested in Chapter 4. The answer might still be 'We don't have a problem', and if so then it is still worth the effort to maintain this good record.

What to do if you and your colleagues do have a problem

Information regarding the problem needs to be collated and analysed.

Data collection

The Library Association suggests

If a problem is identified, then a formal reporting system must be established, as a first step. For this you need a purpose-designed form similar to the widely-used accident report forms. Some authorities have also introduced monthly summary forms. Responsibility for collection and analysis of this information could rest with health and safety supervisors or with managers. It is important that ALL staff are made aware of the proper reporting channels.

(See sample forms on pages 40 and 41).

Data analysis

When the information has been collected it should be analysed to see if it shows whether some kinds of incidents are being repeated. These incidents need to be grouped together into types, each of which will have its own identifying pattern, e.g. harassment from rowdy groups when on late duty. It is through this type of data gathering that particularly vulnerable jobs or tasks can be identified and a search for preventative measures can begin. If you and your colleagues can suggest some solutions then you should inform your managers.

Preventative measures

Management attitude

It is probable that your managers will employ a mixture of preventative measures to achieve control and manage the problem effectively. It is important that these are appropriate and adequate for the task and cost-effective. Staff need to be aware of them and to be trained where appropriate. Installing expensive security hardware, for instance, without changing inadequate systems and procedures, is not likely to be sufficient. Your managers will also need to consider whether the preventative measures could increase the possibility of violence.

The attitude of your managers can drastically affect the reactions of staff and their ability to cope with difficult situations. The Library Association suggests

> A written statement showing sympathy and understanding and containing positive information, eg on insurance protection, can boost the confidence of staff in direct contact with the public. This can be expanded into a 'Help' leaflet, or guidance notes, to be circulated to *all* staff.

Examples of these can be obtained from The Library Association Professional Practice Department.

Communication and consultation

The reporting procedure has been mentioned already but the importance of effective two-way communication cannot be stressed enough.

You must feel able to discuss problems with managers, and managers must consult with staff and trade union representatives at all stages. Some authorities have established working parties to investigate the problem, have produced reporting forms and from the results have made recommendations to senior management or local authority committees. These working parties can include training officers, union representatives, crime prevention officers, community police officers and staff at various levels.

The Library Association gives the following advice:

Opening hours
If it is apparent that incidents occur at set times, e.g. evenings, decisions must be taken on the revision of opening hours. Adjustment to hours may be necessary until the problem is cleared up. Since library users, as well as staff, run the risk of injury or abuse, closure at short notice may be in the best interests of everyone. The reasons for closures should be widely publicized. Opening hours should be under continual review, taking account of lunchtime activity in the area or late night shopping as well as youth club and other community meetings in the evening.

Good working relationships

There are many examples to be seen in various communities where good working relationships with a number of groups can be established to help alleviate some of the problems which may be arising. Contacts with the teachers, head teachers and governors at schools, with police, youth leaders, probation officers, and with other types of libraries and other organizations within the community may be beneficial, through discussing the problems, exchanging information and making a coordinated approach. There could be scope for a committee to include other community workers, meeting either on a regular or *ad hoc* basis. Some libraries have formed user committees who have made a positive contribution to this and other issues.

Informal contact with local police officers can be more productive, and if officers are made aware of the contents of bye-laws etc. they will be better equipped to deal with incidents which they might otherwise regard as outside the remit of the law.

Working environment considerations

The way your workplace is designed and laid out might help to prevent incidents of aggression and violence. Crime prevention officers will advise on the security of existing buildings and – an often overlooked point – on the design of new buildings. A number of organizations have found the following measures decrease the possibility of violence:

➤ Providing clear visibility and lighting for staff so that they can either leave quickly or they can raise help. Ensuring that lighting is adequate both inside and outside the building and in car parks might also help to identify potential assailants. Also making sure that car parks are not too isolated from the information centre/library.

➤ Considering the effects of the locality of the library/information centre. A building shared with other community services with different opening times or near a youth club, a psychiatric unit, or in an area known for disturbances may create some problems for staff and its users.

- ➤ Ensuring that inside the building all parts of the information centre/library can be seen and that the windows can be seen through.
- ➤ The staff entrances and exits need to be safe, particularly for those who are working late. Consider if other safety equipment such as video surveillance equipment is needed. NB *This is particularly necessary for staff such as caretakers and cleaners – they are often in the building outside normal opening hours.*
- ➤ Considering the use of alarms, panic buttons and walkie-talkies.
- ➤ Positioning cash tills away from customers and/or providing physical security at cash tills.
- ➤ Ensuring that the minimum necessary cash and build-up of cash is kept in tills by adopting procedures to move cash quickly and safely to more secure zones.
- ➤ Widening counters and/or raising counter heights on the staff side to give staff more protection (some pubs have done this); relocating the counter if it is in the wrong place; ensuring that the public cannot get behind the counter.
- ➤ Ensuring adequate queue management by using clear and ample signs and, where appropriate, ensuring easy access.
- ➤ Arranging for staff to have access to a secure location and a secure place for personal possessions.
- ➤ Changing the layout of any public areas by providing better seating, lighting and decor.
- ➤ Providing bright lighting around the building and removing possible cover for assailants for staff leaving the building after late duties.
- ➤ Ensuring good quality control on service and systems to defuse any possibility of aggression; providing regular information about any delays.
- ➤ Monitoring high-risk entrances, exits and delivery points.

Before your management undertakes an expensive redesign of the library or information centre, they will need to make sure that it is appropriate to the risk and is relevant to the needs of your work.

There are many ways of making improvements and it is worth examining your physical environment with a critical eye.

The way jobs are designed can reduce the risk of violence. But there are no ready-made remedies; you will have to find measures that are right for your workplace. Here are some examples of measures that have worked for some organizations.

➤ Changing the job to give less face-to-face contact with the public (care should be taken that such measures do not increase the risks of violence to members of the public because there are no visible staff).

➤ Using cheques, credit cards or tokens instead of cash to make robbery less attractive.

➤ Checking the credentials of 'clients' and if possible the place and arrangements for meetings away from the office (this is now standard practice for some estate agents).

➤ Monitoring staffing levels. Even in times of financial constraints it may be necessary to increase staffing levels so that one person is not left alone, especially in the evenings. Alterations in hours can allow this to happen without the need to increase numbers of staff. Security officers may be employed or hired from specialist firms.

➤ Ensuring that staff can get home safely: the threat of violence does not stop when work has ended. The Health and Safety at Work etc. Act requires employers to protect employees while they are at work, but good employers will take further steps where necessary. For example, if your management need staff (particularly female staff) to work late, ask them to try and arrange for staff to be able to drive to work and park their cars in a safe area: many organizations do arrange transport to take their staff home if late hours are required.

➤ Training should be offered, both to give staff more knowledge and confidence in their particular jobs, and to enable them to deal with aggression generally by spotting the early signs of it, by avoiding it or by coping with it.

➤ Installing video cameras or alarm buttons: on buses, for example, cameras have protected staff *and* reduced vandalism and graffiti.

➤ Putting protective screens around staff areas, as in some banks, social security offices and bus drivers' cabs.

➤ Adding 'coded' security locks to doors to keep the public out of staff areas should also be considered.

Staff in mobile libraries may experience particular difficulties in implementing some of the above measures, and should be involved in discussions when security is being considered so that their points of view can be assimilated.

Implementation

Many of the measures outlined above can be implemented with little or no financial outlay and these can be put into practice within a short time scale. Other measures have larger financial considerations and should be incorporated into a rolling programme with appropriate allowance within the budget.

Trades union/staff consultation is crucial at planning, implementation and monitoring stages.

Monitoring

It is essential that the effect of each measure is monitored properly. Effective measures can be identified and sustained; less effective ones replaced or modified. Changes in behaviour patterns can be assessed and policies changed accordingly.

Effective monitoring can also be a valuable method of staff reassurance: if it can be seen that measures are effective, staff morale will be boosted.

Procedures

Revising your working procedures or introducing new methods might help to prevent incidents of violence to staff. Again, a number of organizations have found various measures which are beneficial. These include:

➤ ensuring that staffing levels are appropriate to the particular task and the time of day, and, if there is a high risk, ensuring the level is adequate;

➤ providing adequate and appropriate information to staff on procedures and systems;

➤ ensuring that customer care programmes are adequately designed
and managed; this will be particularly appropriate for dealing with
complaints;

➤ including specific training on violence to staff as part of the health
and safety management training programme (see Chapter 6);

➤ establishing clear emergency procedures, for example, effective
planning for staff on what to do and where to go in the event of an
incident, emergency telephone numbers etc.;

➤ if cash is taken to the bank, varying the times when it is taken and
changing the route: consideration could be given to using professional cash collection services;

➤ ensuring that experienced or less vulnerable staff are used for high-
risk tasks;

➤ rotating high-risk jobs so that the same person is not always at risk,
or doubling up for particularly high-risk tasks;

➤ providing additional staff for high-risk mobile activities or providing communication links to base;

➤ ensuring that details of staff's planned schedules are held by the
base;

➤ providing transport for staff who work alone;

➤ providing personal alarms for high-risk staff;

➤ providing training on recognizing and dealing with violence, and
the potential for violence.

Security systems

These will generally include security equipment specifically designed to
prevent or deter violent crime. Before management decides to install
such equipment, they will consider whether it is appropriate to the risk.
It is pointless to buy expensive and sophisticated CCTV systems if the
risk is minimal. Creating an environment where security is excessive
and impractical should be avoided.

The level and design of equipment will need to take into account:

➤ ease of use by staff;
➤ the pattern and type of business;
➤ the way the building is used, for example when occupied/unoccupied;
➤ whether the geographical location is urban or rural: this may affect the local crime rate; find out what the experience of other businesses in the area is;
➤ the need for emergency access/control.

If you do not have in-house security expertise, you may wish to contact your local police crime prevention officer for advice.

An example quoted from one organization

One library and information centre recognized the possibilities of harm to staff and has issued each member of staff with a personal alarm which when used emits a piercing sound.

All staff have been trained to recognize the warning signals when being confronted by an aggressive customer.

Also, each department and mobile library vehicle has been issued with mobile telephones so as to call immediately if help is needed.

Caring attitude

You and your colleagues will feel that the organization is taking a caring attitude towards you if help is given in various forms described above, and the following may also help:

➤ You will need practical training on how to operate and maintain the security equipment. The equipment will only be as effective as the staff trained to use it.
➤ If you or your colleagues have specific security duties you will need to practise the skills before having to deal with a real event. This will help to build up confidence in the system.

Certain aspects of security procedures should be treated as highly confidential. These details should be given out on a 'need-to-know basis' only. This will help to contain the risk of violence. However, all staff, including part-time or casual workers, will need training in some aspects of security. It may also be useful to display notices so that the public are aware that certain security devices are used in the information centre or library.

Items of equipment such as alarms will need regular maintenance checks to ensure that they are reliable and effective. You and your colleagues will also wish to monitor and evaluate systems to confirm that they are still appropriate. But before your management installs new security equipment to deal with a new threat, consider how it relates to your old security systems.

Points to reflect on . . .

➤ **Do you know what is being done to combat aggression and violence by the various authorities?**

➤ **Do you know which databases to check for further information?**

➤ **Do you know what to do if your management thinks there is not a problem?**

➤ **Name some preventative measures which can be taken.**

Date of incident .... Day of week .... Time ....

EMPLOYEE

Name ....
Address ....
Job/Grade .... Department ....

DETAILS OF ASSAILANT(S)

Name ....
Address ....
Age .... Male/Female ....
Other details ....

WITNESS(ES)

Name ....
Address ....
Age .... Male/Female ....
Other details ....

WHAT HAPPENED?

Give an account of the incident, including any relevant events leading to the incident

----

OUTCOME

Injury? Verbal abuse? Anti-social behaviour? Damage to personal/other property?
Time lost? Legal action?

DETAILS OF LOCATION OF INCIDENT

Provide a sketch if possible

Any other relevant information

Fig. 5.1 *Typical incident report form*

Date of incident .... Day of week .... Time ....

EMPLOYEE

Name .... Library ....

Workplace .... Telephone No ....

Supervisor .... Telephone No ....

What activity were you engaged in at the time of the incident? ....

....

DETAILS OF INCIDENT

Was assault physical or verbal? ....

Location ....

Number of other staff present ....

Was medical assistance/first aid required? ....

Was sick leave required? ....

Injury or stress suffered ....

....

Time lost ....

Legal action ....

Give brief details of incident ....

....

....

Give brief details of assailant (approximate age, height, condition, etc) ....

....

Has the assailant been involved in any previous incident?   YES / NO

Give date and brief details ....

....

Fig. 5.2 *The Library Association incident report form*

Chapter 6
Training: what, where and how?

> **In this chapter you'll find information on:**
>
> ➤ training and refresher training
> ➤ steps to personal safety
> ➤ working alone
> ➤ learning to be an effective communicator
> ➤ actually dealing with aggression and violence.

Training

Training is an important way of achieving competence and helps to convert information into safe working practices. It contributes to your organization's health and safety culture and is needed at all levels, including top management. Risk assessment is required under the terms of The Management of Health and Safety at Work Regulations 1992 Statutory Instrument 1992 No.2051 and will help to determine the level of training needed for each type of work you and your colleagues undertake as part of the preventative and protective measures. So for you this may include basic skills training, specific on-the-job training and training in health and safety or emergency procedures.

Training needs are likely to be greatest on recruitment. If you are a new employee you should receive basic induction training on health and safety, including arrangements for first aid, fire and evacuation. Your organization should also pay particular attention to the needs of young workers. The risk assessment process should indicate further specific training needs. In some cases, training may be required even though an employee already holds formal qualifications.

Changes in your work environment may cause you to be exposed to new or increased risks, requiring further training. The need for further training should be considered when:

1 You or your colleagues transfer or take on new responsibilities and there may be a change in the work activity or in the work environment.

2 There is a change in the work equipment or systems of work in use. A significant change is likely to need a review and re-assessment of risks, which may indicate additional training needs. If the change includes introducing completely new technology, it may bring with it new and unfamiliar tasks. Competent outside advice may be needed.

Refresher training

Your competence will decline if your skills (e.g. in emergency procedures) are not used regularly. Training therefore needs to be repeated periodically to ensure continued competence. Information from personal performance monitoring, health and safety checks, accident investigations and near-miss incidents can help to establish a suitable period for retraining.

If you occasionally deputize for others, consider if you need training in any safety procedures. Your skills are likely to be under-developed and you may need more frequent refresher training.

Training will be an important element in managing and preventing the risk of aggression and violence to staff and should be used to brief you and your colleagues on your organization's policy and procedures; to deliver advice, information and skills on prevention; to involve you and your colleagues in sharing experiences and thoughts on the subject; and as a catalyst to bring about change within your workplace.

The Professional Development Department of The Library Association organizes training courses and workshops on coping with violence and aggression in libraries, as do Victim Support and other organizations (see Appendix A and Appendix D for further details). Watch the professional press for details of courses and seminars.

Steps to personal safety

In addition there are various ways in which you can train yourself as well as learning how to deal with difficult situations and develop communication skills and assertiveness through training. Remember to look confident (even if you do not feel so) because a confident-looking person is less likely to be attacked. You should also keep fit; exercise can help you develop posture, stamina and strength.

Try at all times to avoid confrontation and learn how to do all you can to defuse a potentially violent situation. Should you feel scared or uneasy, act on it straight away and if at all possible move away as confidently and quickly as possible. Should you find yourself in danger, your primary aim is to get away fast, avoiding violence.

Also, be prepared to help if you see someone else in danger. Always remember to ring 999 – if at all possible carry a personal telephone with you.

> **EMERGENCY NUMBER IN THE UK**
> **DIAL 999 – THE CALL IS FREE**

> **When calling the emergency number give as much information as possible including the following:**
>
> • Nature of incident
> • Location of incident
> • Type and seriousness of injuries if any
>
> Remember the following:
>
> • Keep calm, speak clearly and do not hang up until the emergency services have *all* the information they need.
> • Don't wait until an emergency arises – be trained and able to react correctly.
> • No policy or precautions can guarantee the safety of every individual in every situation.

On the move

Sometimes your work can take you to new or unfamiliar locations, e.g. going on training courses, working at another branch location of the information service, attending a conference or a meeting. Make sure someone knows where you are. Leave your schedule behind – train/bus times, hotel name, address, telephone number etc. Know exactly where you are going and how to get there. If your travel plans change, tell your supervisor/colleagues. Make sure you can be contacted. Do you or your organization check out beforehand people you meet alone?

If travelling home after dark, consider all possible risks (e.g. where you parked the car, the availability of public transport, whether anyone is meeting you, etc.). Avoid carrying cash or valuable items. Make sure that valuable items are not too visible or accessible (e.g. laptop or portable computer, mobile phone, briefcase or handbag). Think about carrying a personal alarm or mobile telephone.

Working alone at your usual workplace

If it is necessary to work late-night duties or weekend work will you be working alone? Consider if there are areas where you feel uneasy (e.g. poorly lit entrances or corridors, car parks, etc.), and whether your office/work area might be a potential trap (e.g. possible escape route blocked by a desk, filing cabinet, bookshelves, counter, etc.)?

If you work in a large organization with security staff on 24-hour duty, inform them that you are working late and what time you expect to finish.

Learn to be an effective communicator

Training should make you into an effective communicator and this will help you to reduce considerably the risk of aggressive, or potentially violent, situations developing. It is well known that communication is not just verbal – up to 90% of communication between individuals is non-verbal. So if you are experiencing some form of aggression or bullying from clients or colleagues, work to placate, rather than provoke, them. Learn to talk your way out of problems and if this fails, call upon others

45

to help. *Do not suffer in silence* or you will find yourself becoming tense and stressed, which in itself may increase the other person's aggression.

As we have already seen from the various examples in this book, it is very apparent that aggression and bullying in the workplace is on the increase. Here are a number of useful guidelines you might incorporate on a daily basis (see also overleaf):

➤ Avoid actions which may appear aggressive or may be perceived as an invasion of privacy, e.g. in the desk or work area avoid reading papers or taking any equipment without asking first.

➤ Avoid standing too close/touching someone you work with and avoid over-familiar talk or lewd suggestions.

➤ Do not give your own or colleagues' home telephone numbers or addresses to customers – or anyone else unless there is an agreement to do so. Also, if working in public areas, do not give your personal telephone number when telephoning outside of the organization, because you do not know who else is listening to you!

➤ If anyone in a lift makes you feel uneasy, avoid eye contact, look confident, be on the alert, and get out at the next floor.

➤ It should be possible to avoid after-hours meetings if you are on your own, but if they are unavoidable, ensure that someone knows where you are.

➤ You can dress to please yourself, but bear in mind that society has unwritten rules about appropriate dress for most occupations and situations so wear clothes which give out the signals you intend.

➤ Never get into a car with somebody you do not know and trust.

Actually dealing with aggression

Aggression as defined earlier in the book by various organizations may include *verbal abuse, ostracism, discrimination, racial or sexual harassment, bullying*, etc. You need to be able to assess the situation and decide quickly what actions you should take to contain and curtail this aggression. Training should show you how to deal with a variety of situations, even those which could lead to physical attack. The Consumers' Association policy in Appendix F gives various examples of types of behaviour that might be considered offensive and both informal and formal procedures that might be used to deal with them.

It will be necessary to learn, even if someone is trying to provoke you, not to respond in kind. Meeting aggression with aggression leads to confrontation and someone could get hurt. At all times you must stay calm, speak gently, slowly and clearly. Do not argue or try to outsmart the person verbally. Breathe slowly to control your own tension. Learn how to avoid body language which may be misinterpreted, such as looking down on the aggressor; placing hands on hips, folding or raising arms; using any physical contact. It is advisable to keep your distance.

Also, try to talk through the problem and, however angry you may feel, try to get the person to see your manager or another colleague. If possible allow the person's aggression to be diverted against inanimate objects, such as kicking the counter. Certainly promote compromise by offering the aggressor a way out of the situation.

If you cannot deflect or defuse the situation then get away as quickly and safely as possible. While the incident is taking place keep talking and assess possible ways of escaping if the situation worsens. Try to prevent the aggressor blocking any possible escape route. Never turn your back. If you are trying to get away, move gradually backwards.

After the incident, do learn from it and protect yourself and others from repeated aggressive behaviour. You must therefore report the incident to your immediate supervisor and ensure that your complaint is taken seriously and receives a fair hearing. Fill in the complaints form (see examples on pages 40 and 41).

Physical attack

If you are threatened, you must try not to freeze up but to get away as fast as you can. Aim for a place where you know there will be people, either in your information centre or library or if walking/travelling outside. Do not look back, and report the incident immediately to the police. Someone else might be attacked and may not be able to get away.

If it is not possible to get away, protect yourself and sound your personal alarm if you have one. Shout or scream and give the command

'Phone the police!' or similar positive instruction – people are more likely to react when given a call to action.

As a last resort, the police advice is:

'Bash and Dash' – if you have to fight back, do it quickly. Aim for the knee, solar plexus, elbow joint or little fingers. Then get away.

It is safer to carry a personal alarm than an offensive weapon, which could be used against you.

Self-defence

During your training you will learn that physical self-defence should only be used as the last resort because it limits your options of getting away and will invariably commit you to a fight that you could well lose. Remember also that if you respond physically you could be legally liable for assault.

When an incident occurs

Your management's health and safety policy should give you guidelines on what is acceptable behaviour at work and tell you how to report any incidents. Even with successful implementation of preventative measures, it is inevitable that incidents will still happen and the health and safety guidelines should be drawn up to help staff act when situations do flare up. The following are suggestions for inclusion in the guidelines to be given to all staff:

➤ Do not over-react. However, do not wait until situations get worse – act decisively and positively.
➤ Try to remain calm.
➤ Do not argue or threaten.
➤ Avoid simple mistakes like blocking the exit when asking people to leave.
➤ If you threaten to call the police, call them.
➤ Identify troublemakers and learn their names, tell other colleagues who may have to deal with them on other occasions.
➤ Explain why their actions are unacceptable.

➤ Managers should also decide whether persistent troublemakers should be banned, the exact procedure for making the ban effective and how to inform all concerned.

➤ Managers should clarify under what circumstances staff have the right to close the premises.

➤ All staff should follow the reporting procedure.

Investigations into the problems of aggression and violence at work and its solutions should be carried out continually as part of the risk assessment. You should be aware of the valuable work being done by many trade unions and bodies like the Tavistock Institute of Human Relations. The Library Association continually reviews its work in the field, and collects information on problems and measures. A number of other organizations who can provide help and support are listed in Appendix D.

Training in working hours

Changes in risks may also require changes in the content of training, e.g. where new procedures have been introduced. Health and safety training should take place during working hours. If it is necessary to arrange training outside your normal hours, this should be treated as an extension of time at work.

Training on prevention might include:

➤ Detailing the policy and systems of dealing with the issues.

➤ Recognizing and dealing with abusive and aggressive customers – irrational behaviour, avoiding eye contact, nervousness, hostility, aggressive stance.

➤ Exploring the causes of violence and aggression such as anger and frustration.

➤ Explaining to staff what to do and what is expected of them in the event of aggression, violence and assault including, for example, how to raise the alarm, where to go for safety, and not resisting or following violent offenders.

➤ Managing confrontation by using positive interpersonal skills: listening, remaining calm and confident, being assertive rather than aggressive; defusing situations before they escalate by being non-confrontational and offering a compromise; attracting the attention of colleagues and, if all else fails, ensuring an escape route.

➤ Ensuring effective handling of incidents; letting staff know what to do, who to tell, giving advice on the degree of risk and using role-playing to help staff feel comfortable and confident about security equipment, e.g. panic alarms.

➤ Providing effective customer care; being polite, calm and helpful, recognizing the other person's point of view.

➤ Ensuring safe working practices; if staff are mobile ensuring that someone at the fixed workplace is aware of their exact movements; avoiding where possible working alone or in isolation.

➤ Providing support and care after the incident, including dealing with the impact it can have on staff and making arrangements for support (this will be particularly appropriate for managers and supervisors).

Identifying training needs

Managers of each department/branch will have a key role in identifying the training needs of you and other staff. In particular if you are a manager you will have a management task in controlling and preventing risk. It is therefore important that you are provided with sufficient training on the issue to help you be competent in your management role (this could be part of general management training). And as a manager you may need to consider specific training if you or colleagues move from low-risk to high-risk tasks. All of you will need to be thoroughly briefed on areas of concern to help reduce any foreseeable risk. Where safety representatives are appointed, these should be consulted on training issues.

You should also be aware that training needs in your organization should be monitored and reviewed regularly, and training courses should be evaluated for their effectiveness. Remember, even if you are a part-time worker you will still need the same training as other full-time members of staff.

You and all your colleagues will need to be aware of any risk which you could face while carrying out the job; for example during shift working, mobile work etc. Being aware and able to recognize the potential danger will help you to be prepared. It also ensures that you can react to a situation in a positive way, know what could happen and what would be the best way to deal with it. Training in awareness will include examples of good practice in recognition and effective response. It will also provide you with practical knowledge and information on preventative measures such as systems, procedures and equipment. Awareness can often help to avoid incidents, although it will not always guarantee prevention. Violent incidents will and do happen.

If your management has a policy on apprehending criminals, you and your colleagues will need adequate training and information to ensure that you always act within the law.

Victim support

Your employer may be able to seek assistance and help on training in risk management from the local crime prevention officer. Victim Support will be able to assist with training and providing help and information to staff.

Victim Support is the national charity which provides, through a network of 376 local schemes, emotional support, practical help and information, particularly on the criminal justice system, to victims of crime in England, Wales and Northern Ireland. There is a separate organization for Scotland. The service is confidential and free. Victim Support can also provide information on court procedures and someone to accompany the victim/witness to court if requested. These services are being developed through court-based services in Crown Court centres. The Witness Service offers information and support before, during and after the trial and works in close liaison with local Victim Support schemes and criminal justice agencies. (See the reading list in Appendix A for Victim Support publications.)

Networking

Networking with other libraries or information centres in your area will help to pool knowledge and experience and share information on best practice. It will also help to build a safer working community. It may be that, by networking with similar information services in your area, you and your management are able to set up crime prevention initiatives. Links could also be formed with local commerce and trade associations.

Lessons can be learned from sharing information on styles of management, strategies, systems and the skills required to underpin them. Violence to staff should be a concern to everyone in the area – it could affect you. Depending on the size of your organization, networking can also be useful at regional and national level. It will however be important to agree ground rules for sharing information when it relates to particular security measures used by local libraries or information centres.

Networking could also provide a means of support for anyone who is a victim of serious violent incidents. It helps to prevent isolation and encourages the network to work together in improving the crime rate. Larger libraries will also be in a good position to set standards and help those which may have fewer resources and less information available to them. Crime and violent incidents become rapidly known around the locality, and are often used to judge what the area is like to live and work in. Positive efforts for the community could lead to an improved and safer working environment, and increased profits for local businesses.

The crime prevention officer and the local authority Environmental Health Department will be able to provide you with further information on local crime prevention initiatives and security measures. Some local authorities have crime prevention working groups with councillor representation and involvement. Local Victim Support schemes will be able to offer their service of support and information to staff.

Please note that the information given here is no substitute for training, procedures and practice.

Counselling arrangements

It is essential that counselling must be available for all staff immediately after violent incidents. Staff must receive social and emotional support from immediate superiors, management generally, and any support services available for counselling, including occupational health services.

Points to reflect on . . .

➤ Do you think about the risks at work?

➤ Can you suggest some improvements (even minor changes) to current practice and procedure?

➤ Be vigilant and assess possible risks in your everyday work life, from when you leave home to when you return.

➤ If an incident occurs which requires police assistance, do you know what do?

➤ Have you had any training in dealing with aggression and violence?

Chapter 7
Support you can expect after incidents

> **In this chapter you will learn about:**
>
> ➤ **what help a victim may need**
> ➤ **the immediate support you can expect**
> ➤ **the long-term support.**

As part of your employer's overall health and safety policy, details of responses to staff after an incident involving aggression and violence should be given. Every effort should be made to help to minimize and control any impact on staff and to ensure that they recover from the incident as soon as possible.

It is necessary for the health and safety policy to identify the staff with principal responsibilities at each stage so that all staff are informed of their role and, more importantly, what they should do in case of such incidents.

What about the victims?

Victims may need help. From employers this may include counselling, time off, or help with compensation and legal advice. From work colleagues it may mean giving evidence in court, talking about problems or just being sensitive to the victim's feelings and giving them support.

It is useful to sort out the support you plan to give before an attack happens. Employees will be better able to cope with stressful situations once they know they have their management's support.

If criminal proceedings ensue the Home Office has a useful leaflet called 'Victims of Crime: How can you help the police help you?', which gives information on how to apply for compensation if employees suffer an injury, loss or damage from a crime.

When an incident occurs

When an act of aggression or violence happens it is always a frightening experience because it is unpredictable; the impact on the victim's physical and psychological health can be long lasting and may not immediately be apparent. Consequently support, care and counselling may be needed to help recovery.

Staff may find themselves reacting in various ways which can lead to inefficiency and low morale as well as stress. All these may not be apparent at the time of the incident but may manifest themselves at a later time, so supervisors need to be alert to help the victims.

It is possible that some staff feel anxious about working late, or alone, or do not want to deal with customers known to be awkward or difficult. There is always the fear of assailants or aggressors returning, or worse, waiting for staff to finish work and then following them.

You and colleagues may feel frustrated, angry and helpless and experience loss of confidence and concentration. Other symptoms discussed in earlier chapters will manifest themselves. The main thing is for colleagues, friends and management to be aware that anyone involved in, or at the receiving end of, aggression and violence will need support.

Some staff are so badly affected that the reactions persist, affecting both their personal and professional lives. Training can be helpful in lessening shock and managers will need basic training in dealing with staff during and immediately after an incident, and support and understanding are the key factors in helping staff to recover from a traumatic event. Managers and colleagues will need to know and understand about the impact of shock and how to handle it. They will need the support of their own senior managers on site, and they will need practical operational help if they are expected to keep the information centre or library open.

What to do after an incident has occurred

Some action is necessary as soon as possible after an incident has happened. In addition to private discussion with the victim, an informal group meeting of all those involved peripherally or affected by the incident or individual conversations with an appointed member of staff, may be appropriate. This type of support does not have to be a sophisticated response – sometimes a simple chat and an assessment made that nothing further is needed may be all that is necessary. An immediate response to needs will help staff to feel that what they are going through is a normal reaction and that this need for support is not seen as a failure on their part.

Sometimes group discussions can be particularly effective as a means of sharing experience, concerns and feelings. They can help to ensure that staff do not feel isolated and are aware that there are others with similar reactions and fears. Group discussions can involve those who are directly or indirectly affected. However, their success depends on the willingness of everyone to take part.

It is vital that there is a key person involved with the team who is supportive and has an understanding of the likely impact on the individual. An effective, sensitive initial response is crucial to people's ability to cope in the longer term. It is essential to avoid a situation where staff suffer a loss of self-esteem and are unable to undertake certain tasks or duties.

Staff should be given the opportunity to express their feelings and give:

➤ an outline of the incident (subject to the approval of the victim);
➤ a report on the progress of any investigation or action taken by the management and the police, including what is likely to happen next;
➤ decisions on whether special leave is to be allowed to enable recovery from the incident (this may need to be balanced with encouraging staff to return to 'normality');
➤ legal advice and help in taking proceedings against the assailant.

You and your colleagues should be given what help is needed – both emotional support and practical help – including, if necessary, the rearranging of duties/rosters.

Learning from the feedback on experiences is often helpful in avoiding a recurrence and should be incorporated into the management's policies and action plans.

It is advisable that follow-up action should be taken after a period of time (probably around a month after the incident) to ensure that staff have recovered and do not require additional help. Information and further guidance could also be given on any police action taken, and if appropriate staff need to be prepared for an eventual court case. Victim Support do offer help here and it is worth consulting them.

Long-term support

It is possible that some staff may require extra help and time to overcome their fear, anger and stress, which cannot be provided in the initial response. This should be assessed at follow-up sessions and it may be that counselling or retraining is appropriate.

Should counselling be undertaken 'in-house' it will be important that it is seen to be an independent and confidential service, tailored to the individual circumstances and staff. Otherwise the victim will not feel confident in discussing highly personal and possibly distressing experiences. Counsellors will need to have first-class interpersonal skills – communicating, listening, empathizing, objectivity, tolerance and recognition. It should not be assumed that every member of staff has these qualities, so again it may be that Victim Support can help and provide the services which are needed.

Police action

If it is considered that the incident involves a criminal act, a nominated staff member should immediately contact the police. The reporting procedure (see suggested forms in Chapter 5) should enable a detailed description of the event, offender(s), injuries, etc., to be fully covered.

Local police stations will also know the nearest Victim Support contact. If there is not one locally (double-check your telephone book first), contact the various national headquarters of Victim Support (see Appendix D, p. 67). You will also find useful guidance in the HSE booklet *Preventing violence to staff* mentioned earlier (p.28).

Points to reflect on . . .

➤ If an incident occurred would you know how to help the victim immediately?
➤ What other support could be considered?
➤ Have you read some of the extra guidance available from the various authorities, e.g. the Health and Safety Executive?

Appendix A
Bibliography

Arranged alphabetically by authors, these publications will help with further information and offer ideas for training and training courses. Please see Appendix D for addresses.

Adams, A., *Bullying at work: how to confront and overcome it*, London, Virago Press, 1992.

Cardy, C. and Lamplugh, D., *Training for personal safety at work*, 1994 (available in paperback and looseleaf binder format).

Cox, T. for the Health and Safety Executive, *Stress research and stress management: putting theory to* work, Sudbury, HSE, Contract Research Report 61, (PO Box 1999, Sudbury, Suffolk CO10 6FS. Tel: +44 (0) 1787 881165. Fax: +44 (0) 1787 313995), 1993.

Craig, M. and Phillips, E., *Office workers' survival handbook: a guide to fighting health hazards in the office*, Women's Press, 1991.

Department of Health, *ABC of mental health in the workplace*, Department of Health, 1995.

Department of Transport, *Crime on the London Underground*, report of a study by Department of Transport in conjunction with London Underground, the Home Office, the Metropolitan Police and British Transport Police, Department of Transport, Nov. 1986.

Department of Transport and the Suzy Lamplugh Trust with the cooperation of London Underground Ltd, the Bus and Coach Council and the British Transport Police, *Travel safely by public transport*, 1995 (available from Department of Transport and The Suzy Lamplugh Trust).

Hazards, 'Bullying at work', *Hazards*, **48** (2), Autumn 1994.

Health and Safety Authority, *Violence at work*, HSA, 1995.

Health and Safety Executive, *5 steps to risk assessment*, IND(G) 163L, Sudbury, HSE Books, (PO Box 1999, Sudbury, Suffolk CO10 6FS. Tel: +44 (0) 1787 881165. Fax: +44 (0) 1787 313995), 1992.

Health and Safety Executive, *Preventing violence to retail staff*, HS(G) 133, Sudbury, HSE Books, (PO Box 1999, Sudbury, Suffolk CO10 6FS. Tel: +44 (0) 1787 881165. Fax: +44 (0) 1787 313995), 1992.

Health and Safety Executive, *Prevention of violence to staff in banks and building societies*, HS(G) 100, Sudbury, HSE Books, (PO Box 1999, Sudbury, Suffolk CO10 6FS. Tel: +44 (0) 1787 881165. Fax: +44 (0) 1787 313995), 1993.

Health and Safety Executive, *Stress at work: a guide for employers*, HS(G) 116, Sudbury, HSE Books, (PO Box 1999, Sudbury, Suffolk CO10 6FS. Tel: +44 (0) 1787 881165. Fax: +44 (0) 1787 313995), 1995.

Health and Safety Executive, *Violence to staff*, IND(G) 69L, Sudbury, HSE Books, (PO Box 1999, Sudbury, Suffolk CO10 6FS. Tel: +44 (0) 1787 881165. Fax: +44 (0) 1787 313995), 1995.

The Library Association, *Violence in libraries: preventing aggressive and unacceptable behaviour in libraries*, The Library Association, Manpower and Education Division, June 1987.

MSF, *Bullying at work: how to tackle it: a guide for MSF representatives and members*, Bishops Stortford, MSF Health and Safety Office, August 1995.

Overall, S., 'Union demands action to stop bullying at work', *People management*, **10**, 21 September 1995.

Overall, S., 'HSE tightens its line on violence in the workplace', *People management*, **8–9**, 5 October 1995.

Poyner, B., 'The prevention of violence to staff', *Journal of health and safety*, **1**, July 1988, 19–26.

Poyner, B., 'Working against violence', *Occupational health*, **41** (8), August 1989, 209–11.

Poyner, B. and Ware, C. for the Health and Safety Executive and Tavistock Institute of Human Relations, *Violence to staff: a basis for assessment and prevention*, Sudbury, HSE Books, (PO Box 1999, Sudbury, Suffolk CO10 6FS. Tel: +44 (0) 1787 881165. Fax: +44 (0) 1787 313995), 1986.

Poyner, B. and Warne, C. for the Health and Safety Executive and Tavistock Institute of Human Relations, *Preventing violence to staff*, Sudbury, HSE Books, (PO Box 1999, Sudbury, Suffolk CO10 6FS. Tel: +44 (0) 1787 881165. Fax: +44 (0) 1787 313995), 1988.

Reynolds, P., *Dealing with crime and aggression at work: a handbook for organizational action*, McGraw-Hill, 1994. (This book has some extensive training programmes in it to help staff manage aggressive and abusive incidents more effectively.)

The Suzy Lamplugh Trust, *Beating aggression*, London, Suzy Lamplugh Trust, 1995.

The Suzy Lamplugh Trust, *Living safety*, London, Suzy Lamplugh Trust, 1995.

The Suzy Lamplugh Trust, *The pocket fast guide to personal safety at work*, London, Suzy Lamplugh Trust/Hascombe Enterprises Ltd, 1995.

Trades Union Congress, 'Violence to staff: report on recent work', *Trades Union Congress health and safety bulletin*, 8, 1988, 9–11.

Appendix B
Legislation

Legislation and guides to legislation from the UK

Health and Safety at Work etc. Act 1974, Ch 37, HMSO

About the legislation

The Health and Safety at Work etc. Act 1974 (HSW Act) puts broad general responsibilities on you as an employer and others to protect the health and safety of staff. In particular, section 2 of the HSW Act gives employers a duty to safeguard, so far as is reasonably practicable, the health, safety and welfare at work of their staff.

Employers also have a common-law general duty of care towards their staff, which extends to the risk of violence at work. Legal precedents (see *West Bromwich Building Society v Townsend* (1983) IRLR 147 and *Charlton v Forrest Printing Ink Company Limited* (1980) IRLR 331) show that employers have a duty to take reasonable care to see that their staff are not exposed to unnecessary risks at work including the risk of injury by criminals. In carrying out their duty to provide a safe system of work and a safe working place, employers should, therefore, have regard to, and safeguard their staff against, the risk of injury from violent criminals.

Guide

Health and Safety Executive, *A guide to the Health and Safety at Work etc. Act 1974*. Series L1. 5th edn, 1992. Sudbury, Suffolk, HSE Books, (PO Box 1999, Sudbury, Suffolk CO10 6FS. Tel: +44 (0) 1787 881165. Fax: +44 (0) 1787 313995).

The Management of Health and Safety at Work Regulations 1992
Statutory Instrument, 1992, No. 2051, HMSO

About the legislation

The Management of Health and Safety at Work Regulations 1992 require employers to assess the risks to the health and safety of their staff and of anyone else who may be affected by their work activity. This is so that the necessary preventative and protective measures can be identified. Employers must also make arrangements for putting into practice the health and safety measures that follow from their risk assessment. The measures will have to cover planning, organisation, control monitoring and review, in other words, the management of health and safety.

Guide

Health and Safety Executive, *Management of Health and Safety at Work Regulations 1992, Approved code of practice, Series L21*, (PO Box 1999, Sudbury, Suffolk CO10 6FS. Tel: +44 (0) 1787 881165. Fax: +44 (0) 1787 313995), 1992.

The Reporting of Injuries, Diseases and Dangerous Occurrences Regulations 1995

About the legislation

This regulation has been streamlined and provides for reporting of incidents of violence in the workplace.
Statutory Instrument 1995, No. 3163, 6 December 1995, HMSO.

The Safety Representatives and Safety Committees Regulations 1977

Statutory Instrument 1977, no. 500, as amended by SI 1992, no. 2051, HMSO.

About the legislation

The Safety Representatives and Safety Committees Regulations (SRSC) 1977 provide that a recognized independent trade union may appoint safety representatives to represent employees in consultation with employers on promoting, developing and monitoring measures to ensure health and safety at work. The Schedule within the Management of Health and Safety at Work Regulations 1992 amended the SRSC Regulations to require employers to consult safety representatives 'in good time' over a range of health and safety issues.

Guide

Health and Safety Executive., Safety representatives and safety committees, 1988 (The Brown Book). Series COP 1 (PO Box 1999, Sudbury, Suffolk CO10 6FS. Tel: +44 (0) 1787 881165. Fax: +44 (0) 1787 313995).

Swedish legislation

Swedish National Board of Occupational Safety and Health, Ordinance on victimisation at work, ASF, 1993, 17. Swedish National Board of Occupational Safety and Health, S-171 84 Solna, Sweden.

Appendix C
Databases

HSELINE, CISDOC and **NIOSHTIC** are databases available on the compact disc **OSHROM** from SilverPlatter Information Ltd. These are leading bibliographic databases covering occupational health and safety information:

➤ NIOSHTIC, from the US National Institute for Occupational Safety and Health, which covers occupational health and safety topics from the United States and elsewhere;

➤ HSELINE, from the Health and Safety Executive, covering occupational health and safety issues in the United Kingdom and from worldwide sources;

➤ CISDOC, from the International Occupational Safety and Health Information Centre of the UN International Labour Organisation, also covering worldwide sources.

They contain a wealth of information on aggression, bullying and violence in the workplace. The references are to legislation, guidance and advice, leaflets, reports, journal articles, translations and research reports.

OSHROM is available for a 30 days' free trial from SilverPlatter, who will also send details of the compact disc OSH-CD which contains the full text of all Health and Safety Executive and Commission publications and all health and safety legislation.

OSH-CD gives unlimited access to essential health and safety information, stored on one CD-ROM instantly accessible at the touch of a key, from the UK Health and Safety Executive, HMSO and SilverPlatter.

It contains the *full text* of:

➤ appropriate health and safety legislation;
➤ appropriate Statutory Instruments;
➤ guidance and advice;
➤ newsletters and journals

plus abstracts from British Standards.

The references produced by the HSE/C quoted in the reading list are available full text in OSH-CD.

For more information on OSH-CD and OSHROM, or to become a SilverPlatter Subscriber, you can contact:

Silverplatter Information Ltd
10 Barley Mow Passage
Chiswick, London W4 4PH
Tel: 0800 262 096
+44 (0) 81 995 8242
Fax: +44 (0) 81 995 5159

SilverPlatter Information Ltd
10 River Ridge Drive
Norwood MA 02062-5043
Tel: 800 343 0064
+1 617 769 2599
Fax: +1 617 769 8763

or via the Internet at: info@SilverPlatter.com

Appendix D
Contacts for help

Association of Personal Injury Lawyers
10a Byard Lane
Nottingham NG1 2GJ
Tel: +44(0)115 958 0585
Fax: +44(0)115 958 0885
The Association has over 2,500 members able to give medical and legal advice; represents special plaintive work.

British Association for Counselling
1 Regent Place
Rugby
Warwickshire CV21 2PJ
Tel: +44(0)178 857 8328
Fax: +44(0)178 856 2189
Offers guidance and advice.

Citizens Advice Bureaux
Check your local telephone directory for local number.
Offers guidance and advice.

Health and Safety Agency
22 North Street
Belfast BT1 1NW
Tel: +44(0)123 224 3249
Fax: +44(0)123 223 5383
Offers health and safety guidance and advice to those suffering work-place aggression and violence.

Health and Safety Authority
10 Hogan Place
Dublin 2
Ireland
Tel: +353 1 662 0400
Fax: +353 1 662 0411
Offers health and safety guidance and advice to those suffering workplace aggression and violence.

Health and Safety Executive
Information Centre
Broad Lane
Sheffield S3 7HQ
Tel: +44(0)114 289 2345
Fax: +44(0)114 289 2333
Offers health and safety guidance and advice to those suffering workplace aggression and violence.

Irish Association of Victim Schemes
29–30 Dane Street
Dublin 2
Ireland
Tel: +353-1 679 8673
Fax: +353-1 679 3839
Offers guidance and advice to victims of aggression and violence.

The Library Association
Professional Practice Department
7 Ridgmount Street
London WC1E 7AE
Tel: +44(0)171 636 7543
Fax: +44(0)171 436 7218
e-mail: info@la-hq.org.uk.
Professional body for information and library staff; offers advice, guidance and training.

MSF Health and Safety Office
Whitehall College
Dane O'Coys Road
Bishops Stortford
Herts CM23 2JN
Tel: +44(0)171 378 7255
Fax: +44(0)171 378 1896
Offers health and safety guidance and advice to those suffering work-place aggression and violence.

The Samaritans
10 The Grove
Slough
Berkshire SL1 1QP
Tel: +44(0)175 353 2713
Fax: +44(0)175 352 4332
or check your local telephone directory for local number.
Offers guidance and advice.

The Suzy Lamplugh Trust
14 East Sheen Avenue
London SW14 8AS
Tel: +44(0)181 392 1839
Fax: +44(0)181 392 1830
Offers guidance and advice, particularly for those who work alone.

Trades Union Congress (TUC)
Health and Safety Office
Congress House
23 Great Russell Street
London WC1B 3LS
Tel: +44(0)171 636 4030
Fax: +44(0)171 636 0632
Offers health and safety guidance and advice to those suffering work-place aggression and violence.

Trauma After-Care Trust
Buttfields
The Farthings
Withington
Gloucestershire GL54 4DF
Tel: +44(0)124 289 0306
Fax: +44(0)124 289 0498
A charity to help people suffering from the psychological after-effects of trauma.

Trauma Stress Service
Maudsley Hospital
Denmark Hill
Camberwell
London SE5 8AB
Tel: +44(0)171 919 2969
Offers a UK-wide service in counselling. Initially linked with a range of major disasters, but the bulk of the work is with lower-profile cases.

Victim Support
National Office
Cranmer House
39 Brixton Road
London SW9 6DZ
Tel: +44(0)171 735 9166
Victim Support is the national charity which helps crime victims. Service is confidential and free.

In Northern Ireland
Victim Support Northern Ireland
Annsgate House
70–74 Ann Street
Belfast BT1 4EH
Tel: +44(0)123 224 4039
Fax: +44(0)123 231 3838

In Scotland
Victim Support Scotland
14 Frederick Street
Edinburgh
Scotland
Tel: +44(0)131 225 7779
Fax: +44(0)131 225 8456

In Wales
Victim Support
1a Victoria Park Road
Victoria Park
Cardiff CF5 1E2
Tel: +44(0)122 257 8392
Fax: +44(0)122 257 8824

Appendix E
Videos and films

There are a number of training videos and films, many of which are listed below. The first item is a catalogue of resources available.

Audiovisual resources in occupational health and safety, Health and Safety Executive: films, videos and tape slides available from distributors in the United Kingdom. 1995, ISBN 0 7176 0960 X. Price £15.00.
(Available from HSE Books, PO Box 1999, Sudbury, Suffolk CO10 6FS, UK. Tel: +44(0)178 788 1165. Fax: +44(0)178 731 3995, or through good booksellers.)

Aggression at work: a series of three videos directed at those people coping with individuals dealing with or diffusing aggression in the workplace; Part 1 – the problem from a management responsibility point of view; Part 2 – what employees can do to help matters; Part 3 – ways of dealing with actual violence. Sale: Part 1 £315.00, Parts 2 and 3 £290.00 each. 20–27mins each.
(Videotel International, Ramilies House, 1/2 Ramilies Street, London W1V 1DF. Tel: +44(0)171 439 6301. Fax: +44(0)171 437 0731.)

Coping with violence and aggression. Sale: £47.00. Hire: 28 days £14.00. 12mins. Graves Medical Audiovisual.
(Leeds University Audiovisual Services, Television Centre, Leeds LS2 9JT, UK. Tel: +44(0)113 243 1751 ext 6440.)

Dealing with conflict and confrontation: how to keep your cool, stand your ground and reach a positive solution. Video and audio include: 40 page workbook. Each additional workbook (V10145B) is £9.50.
(CareerTrack Publications, Sunrise House, Sunrise Parkway, Linford Wood, Milton Keynes MK14 6YA, UK. Tel: +44(0)190 834 5000. Fax: +44(0)190 867 9931.)

How to deal with difficult people: strategies for getting results with the hard-to-handle people in your life. 4 audiocassettes (3hrs, 26mins), V10015,

£59.95. 3 volume video set (4hrs, 20mins), V20380. Video includes 32 page workbook, each additional workbook (V20034B) is £7.50.

(CareerTrack Publications, Sunrise House, Sunrise Parkway, Linford Wood, Milton Keynes MK14 6YA, UK. Tel: +44(0)190 834 5000. Fax: +44(0)190 867 9931.)

Difficult people video plus *Conflict video*.

V20832, £325.00 (includes workbooks).

(CareerTrack Publications, Sunrise House, Sunrise Parkway, Linford Wood, Milton Keynes MK14 6YA, UK. Tel: +44(0)190 834 5000. Fax: +44(0)190 867 9931.)

In the face of aggression: the external threat

The first part of this film shows seven distinct dramatized scenes typifying the various kinds of aggression which might be encountered in the course of a days work. Part 2 analyses these incidents and shows how to defuse an awkward or menacing situation.

Sale: £845.00. Hire: 2 days £140.00, 5 days £180.00. Part 1: 22mins. Part 2: 20mins.

(Fenman Training, Clive House, The Business Park, Ely, Cambridgeshire CB7 4EH. Tel: 01353 665533. Fax: 01353 663644.)

Interpersonal communication skills: training to minimize conflict and build collaboration in today's team-oriented workplace

4 audiocassettes (4hrs, 19mins), V10178, £59.95. 4 volume video set (5hrs, 23mins), V20733, £249.95. Audio and video include: 40 page workbook, each additional workbook (V10178B) is £9.50.

(CareerTrack Publications, Sunrise House, Sunrise Parkway, Linford Wood, Milton Keynes MK14 6YA, UK. Tel: +44(0)190 834 5000. Fax: +44(0)190 867 9931.)

Sexual harassment: how to protect yourself and your organisation, with Maria Arapkis

3 volume video set (2hrs, 6mins), V20477, £349.95. Includes a 40 page workbook, each additional workbook (V20470B) is £9.50.

(CareerTrack Publications, Sunrise House, Sunrise Parkway, Linford Wood, Milton Keynes MK14 6YA, UK. Tel: +44(0)190 834 5000. Fax: +44(0)190 867 9931.)

Appendix F
Example of anti-harassment policy from the Consumers' Association

Consumers' Association Anti-Harassment Policy

Anti-harassment policy

CA's Philosophy and Mission states that we need to 'conduct working relationships with fairness, courtesy and respect', and that 'our people are our main resource'. CA is committed to protecting all its staff from harassment: all incidents of harassment are unacceptable and will not be tolerated. For the purpose of this paper the terms 'staff' and 'colleague' include all managers and non managerial staff.

In order to support the organisation's philosophy, to demonstrate good employment practice, and to meet legal and moral requirements an anti-harassment policy has been devised in conjunction with the Joint Union (MSF and NUJ). It is supported by the Staff Association.

This document sets out the CA policy on harassment and outlines the procedure to follow if any member of staff feels that they have been subjected to harassment. The policy applies to all members of staff during working hours, and outside normal hours where an individual's action detrimentally affects the organisation or a CA colleague.

All staff have a duty to be aware of how their behaviour affects others: what matters is how it feels to the individual on the receiving end of the behaviour; they decide what is acceptable to them and what is not. CA recognises that there may be cases where a member of staff may be unaware of the effect of their behaviour on colleagues. For this reason, it is particularly important that staff familiarise themselves with this policy and be aware of the possible effects of their conduct on other colleagues.

This agreement is designed to promote awareness amongst staff of the reasonableness or otherwise of what may or may not be acceptable behaviour to colleagues. This policy provides two means of dealing with complaints of harassment: an informal procedure and a formal procedure. The formal procedure will enable a judgement to be made on the merits of a complaint, and if a complaint is upheld disciplinary action will follow. An appeal process is available – to both complainant and alleged harasser – should either party feel that they have been unfairly treated.

All staff have a responsibility to be aware that there is a distinction between consensual behaviour and conduct which is not desired by another colleague. Any member of staff who feels that they are being harassed should not hesitate to use the procedures set out below.

Disciplinary action will be taken against those whose behaviour is contrary to the policy. Harassment in any form, could constitute gross misconduct and lead to dismissal. Similarly, any unwarranted allegation of harassment, made in bad faith and with malicious intent, may also be regarded as gross misconduct and could lead to dismissal.

In their specific line management role, managers have a special duty to be vigilant of the behaviour of individuals within their teams, and are responsible for addressing actions which might cause offence. Managers are expected to act before waiting for a complaint to be registered.

What is harassment?

Harassment is behaviour which is unwanted, unreciprocated and offensive to another

Harassment takes many forms and includes physical, verbal or non verbal conduct. It can include comments, actions, jokes or suggestions which may create a stressful working environment. Harassment is often sexual or racial but can be for any other reason: such as someone simply taking a personal dislike to a colleague; or making comments on the grounds of a colleague's sexual orientation; or derogatory comments about a colleague's disability, religion or age. Harassment can be related to a colleague's position in the organisation – for example a person in position of authority abusing that power and displaying an intimidating management style. Harassment may be an isolated incident or repeated action.

Examples of harassment

CA will not permit harassment in any form, whether this is harassment based on gender, race, religion, colour, ethnic or national origin, age, disability, political conviction, membership or non-membership of a trade union, status of ex-offenders, real or suspected infection with HIV/Aids, marital or health status, sexual preference, bullying or willingness to challenge harassment.

Further examples of harassment are listed in more detail below, but this is not exhaustive.

The following are examples of bullying:

➤ shouting at a colleague; persistently negative attacks on a colleague's personal or professional performance; criticizing a colleague in front of others;
➤ spreading malicious rumours/making malicious allegations;
➤ persistently setting objectives with impossible deadlines or unachievable tasks;
➤ removing and replacing areas of responsibility with menial or trivial tasks;
➤ undervaluing a colleague's contribution; placing unreasonable demands on and/or over-monitoring a colleague's performance;
➤ withholding information with the intent of deliberately affecting a colleague's performance;
➤ excluding colleagues by talking solely to third parties to isolate another.

Line managers are responsible for ensuring that the staff who report to them perform to an acceptable standard. Bullying does not therefore include legitimate, justifiable, appropriately conducted criticism of an employee's behaviour or job performance.

The following are examples of sexual harassment:

➤ unwanted, non-accidental physical contact ranging from unnecessary touching, patting, pinching, or brushing against a colleague's body, to assault and coercing sexual relations;
➤ unwelcome sexual advances, propositions or pressure for sexual activity, continued suggestions for social activity within or outside

the workplace, after it has been made clear that such suggestions are unwelcome, and offensive flirting;

➤ suggestions that sexual favours may further a colleague's career or refusal may hinder it, e.g. promotions, salary increases etc.;

➤ the display of pornographic or sexually suggestive pictures, objects or written materials;

➤ leering, whistling or making sexually-suggestive comments or gestures, innuendoes or lewd comments;

➤ conduct that denigrates or ridicules or is intimidatory or physically abusive of an employee because of his or her sex, such derogatory or degrading abuse or insults which are gender-related and offensive comments about appearance or dress.

The following are examples of racial harassment:

➤ conduct that denigrates or ridicules a colleague because of his or her race, (such as derogatory remarks, graffiti, jokes); such conduct can be verbal, non verbal or physical;

➤ the display or sending of offensive letters or publications, racist graffiti or threatening behaviour;

➤ being 'frozen out' of conversations, jostling or assault, or other non-accidental physical contact;

➤ derogatory nicknames or racial name calling.

Procedures

What to do if you feel you are being bullied, or have been harassed

Many people subjected to harassment do not complain because they feel embarrassed; they are worried that they will be victimized, or they don't want to get the other person into trouble.

CA guarantees that all complaints will be taken seriously and investigated swiftly, and that all parties involved will be treated with respect. Victimization as a result of a member of staff raising a complaint will not be tolerated and will be treated as harassment and subject to disciplinary action. Likewise, staff shall be protected from victimization or discrimination for assisting in an investigation.

The following is an outline of the informal and formal procedures to be taken when dealing with harassment issues.

If you feel you are being harassed you may find it helpful to have a confidential discussion with a CA trained counsellor, to help you decide on how best to progress the matter further. A cross-section of CA staff have been trained to help you. Their names and extension numbers are listed on the sheet attached to this policy. Any contact that you have with them is *strictly confidential*. They will provide in-confidence advice and will assist in the resolution of any problems, whether through informal or formal means. Whichever means (formal or informal) you choose to deal with the issue *you should keep a record of events*.

The informal procedure

Stage one

If an incident happens which offends you and leads you to believe you are being harassed, you should initially attempt to resolve the problem informally, with the help if you wish it of one of the counsellors. Counsellors are staff recruited from a cross-section of the organisation who have received special training. In some cases if may be possible and sufficient to explain clearly to the person engaging in the unwanted conduct that the behaviour in question is not welcome; that it offends you or makes you feel uncomfortable, and that it interferes with your work.

In circumstances where this is too difficult or too embarrassing for you to do on your own you should seek support from one of the trained counsellors, a JU or SA representative, a Personnel Officer or a friend.

If you are in any doubt as to whether an incident, or series of incidents, which have occurred to you constitute harassment, then in the first instance you should not hesitate to approach the trained counsellors for confidential advice, on an informal basis. They will be able to advise you as to whether the incident merits further action and if so how the matter may be dealt with.

Many incidents of harassment can be dealt with effectively in an informal way, as often the harasser has no idea of the effect their behaviour is having on others. Once it is drawn to their attention their behaviour ceases.

However, if the problem persists, or if you prefer, the following steps can be taken.

The formal procedure

Stage two

➤ You should register a formal complaint against the alleged harasser. Your complaint should be put in writing to your Personnel Officer, outlining the nature of the complaint. Your counsellor or staff representative will help you to do this if you wish, but you have the right to initiate a formal complaint without reference to a counsellor first. If your chosen counsellor is also your Personnel Officer, you may register the formal complaint to the Personnel Manager, to ensure fairness. In some cases involving a senior member of staff the Personnel Officer's place may be taken by the Personnel Manager or Director of Human Resources. Throughout the formal process your name and the name of the alleged harasser will not be divulged other than to those who are necessary to the investigation.

➤ The formal complaint will be treated as a disciplinary issue and will be investigated following CA's disciplinary procedure.

➤ A timetable will be set down for the investigation.

➤ There will be an independent investigation carried out by the Personnel Officer involved in the complaint, to establish the full details of what has happened. You will be interviewed, as will the alleged harasser. Separate interviews will be conducted. Your counsellor or representative will provide help and support during this process if you wish.

➤ The investigation will be thorough, impartial and objective. It will be carried out with sensitivity and with due respect for the rights of both the complainant and the alleged harasser.

The complainant and the alleged harasser will have the right to be accompanied at all interviews. The alleged harasser will be given full details of the nature of the complaint and will be given the opportunity to respond. They will also have access to a counsellor. The investigatory meeting will be held separately and will not be confrontational. Every effort will be made to ensure that the meeting is conducted sensitively.

Strict confidentiality will be maintained throughout the investigation into the allegation. Where it is necessary to interview witnesses, the importance of confidentiality will be emphasised. It will be explained to witnesses that any breach of confidence would constitute gross misconduct under CA's disciplinary rules and would itself be subject to disciplinary action.

➤ At the completion of the investigation a short report will be prepared summarising the details of the complaint, the results of the investigation and the conclusion. A copy will be sent to both the complainant and the alleged harasser.

➤ If the investigation indicates that harassment has taken place, the harasser will be subject to a disciplinary interview. Depending on the circumstances and the seriousness of the complaint, an appropriate penalty will be applied.

➤ If you feel you have been unfairly treated during this procedure you have the right to lodge an appeal to the director. Ultimately you can take your complaint to an Industrial Tribunal.

The author is indebted to Emma Murray, Consumers' Association (2 Marylebone Road, London NW1 4DX, Tel: 0171 486 5544, Fax: 0171 935 1606), for permission to use this policy as an example for others to follow.

Index